The Quran

SELECTED PASSAGES WITH INTERPRETED MEANINGS A PRAGMATIC AND CONTEXTUAL TRANSLATION APPROACH

SECOND EDITION

Dr. Yunus J. Kumek

Sage Chronicle $^\lambda$
publishing house

Cover image: Shutterstock.com
Interior background: Shutterstock.com

Sage Chronicle $^\lambda$
publishing house
www.sagechronicle.org
3380 Sheridan Drive, #240
New York 14226
contact@sagechronicle.org

Copyright © 2019, 2020 by Sage Chronicle$^\lambda$ Publishing House

ISBN 978-1-951050-11-5

All rights reserved. No part of this publication may be reproduced, stored in a retrieval system, or transmitted, in any form or by any means, electronic, mechanical, photocopying, recording, or otherwise, without the prior written permission of the copyright owner.

Published in the United States of America.

BRIEF CONTENTS

Part 1

Introduction to Islam with Questions and Answers

Part 2

Selected Passages from Each Chapter of the Quran with Interpreted Meanings and Discussion Questions

Part 3

Preferred Translation Methodology of the Quran

CONTENTS

Preface xxiii

Part 1: Introduction to Islam with Questions and Answers 1

Why do we need to know about Islam? 2
How was Islam started? 2
Who is Allah? 2
   Different Names (Attributes) of Allah, God *3*
Who is the Prophet Muhammad? 7
What is the Quran? 9
   Authenticity of the Quran *12*
What do Muslims believe? 14
   Six Articles of Faith in Islam *14*
Who is God for Muslims? 14
   The Belief in the Creator *14*
   God: The Divine and the Creator *15*
Why is belief in one God the core of Islam? 16
How do Muslims understand miracles? 17
   Miracles *17*
Who is a prophet or messenger in Islam? 18
   Believing in Prophets *18*
Do the Muslims believe in the Bible, Psalms, and Torah? 24
   Belief in the Divine Books *24*
Are the angels in Islam similar to those in Christianity and Judaism? 26
   Belief in Angels *26*
What happens after death? 27
   Life after Death *27*

What is the understanding of evil, good, and destiny? 28
   Destiny, Evil, and Good...28
What are the worship requirements in Islam? 29
   Five Worship Pillars of Islam..29
Who is considered a Muslim? 29
   Declaration of Faith..29
What are the daily prayers in Islam? 31
   Five Times Daily Prayer 31
What is Ramadan? 33
   Fasting 33
Are Muslims required to give charity?............................... 34
   Charity 34
What is the Muslim's pilgrimage or Hajj? 34
   Pilgrimage 34
   The Kabah 34
What are the similarities and differences between Islam,
   Judaism, and Christianity? 36
   Comparing Islam with Christianity, Judaism, and other Religions 36
Are the Muslims in America and Europe different?.................. 37
   Islam in the West..37
What is the place of societal customs and culture in Islam?............ 39
   Customs and Culture...39
Are Muslims violent? 39
   Violence 39
What is Islamic Law? 41
   Law, Society, and Politics...41
What is Sufism? 42
   Sufism...42
What is the role of women in Islam? 44
   Women..44
How are the contemporary social ethics issues viewed? 47
   Social Ethics...47
What is the place of Art, Education, and Science in Islam? 49
   Art, Education, and Science 49
What is Halal? 51
   The Muslim's Diet: Permissible and Impermissible 51

Part 2: Selected Passages from Each Chapter of the Quran with Interpretive Meanings and Discussion Questions .. 53

The Names of Chapters in the Quran..............................54
Table of Different Names of the Quran 58
Notes on Transliteration and Translated Interpretive Meanings.........61

1. **The Opening**...64
   The Opening..64
       Commentary..65
       Discussion Questions 65
2. **This Book**..66
   This Book 66
       Commentary..67
       Discussion Questions 67
   God..67
       Commentary..68
       Discussion Questions 69
   The Friend and the Friend 69
       Commentary..70
       Discussion Questions:.....................................70
   Everyone...70
       Commentary..71
       Discussion Questions 71
3. **Common Word**...72
   Family of Jesus 72
       Discussion Question 72
   Adam and Jesus...72
       Discussion Questions 72
   Common Word 73
       Discussion Questions 73
   Rotation of Days 73
       Discussion Questions 74
4. **Creation in Pairs** 75
   Creation in Pairs 75
       Commentary..75
       Discussion Question 75

Does God oppress? 76
    Discussion Questions 76
Pure Belief 76
    Discussion Question 77
Don't they think about this Quran? 77
    Discussion Questions 77
The Etiquette of Greeting.. 77
    Discussion Question 77
More Truthful Words... 78
    Discussion Question 78
Hiding from Who?.. 78
    Discussion Question 78

5. **Conflict and Justice** 79
    Conflict and Justice 79
        Discussion Question 79
    The Prophet, the Quran, and the Followers of the Bible: the Gospel,
        the Psalms, and the Torah and the Educated People............. 79
        Discussion Questions 80

6. **Ecosystem and Species** 81
    Knowing about the Prophet with Certainty...................... 81
        Discussion Question 81
    Lying against Their Own Selves 81
        Discussion Question 81
    Ecosystem and Species... 82
        Discussion Question 82
    Appreciating the Scriptures Revealed by God 82
        Discussion Question 83

7. **Doing the evil and blaming others?**............................ 84
    Doing the evil and blaming others? 84
        Discussion Questions 84

8. **Uniting the Hearts** 85
    Uniting the Hearts... 85
        Discussion Question 85

Contents

9. Trade 86
   Trade 86
      Commentary 86
      Discussion Question 86
   Categories 87
      Discussion Question 87

10. Will you force people to believe? 88
   Will you force people to believe? 88
      Discussion Questions 88
   Alternation of Night and Day 88
      Discussion Question 88

11. Continuous Struggle 89
   Continuous Struggle 89
      Discussion Questions 89

12. Language of the Revelation 90
   Language of the Revelation 90
      Discussion Question 90
   The Best Story 91
      Commentary 91
      Discussion Question 91

13. Moving the Mountains, Splitting the Earth, and Speaking with the Dead 92
   Moving the Mountains, Splitting the Earth, and Speaking with the Dead 92
      Discussion Questions 92

14. A Nice Word and a Nice Tree 93
   A Simple Good Word and a Nice, Strong Tree 93
      Discussion Questions 93

15. Upgraded and Downgrade 94
   I Wish 94
      Discussion Question 94
   Upgraded and Downgraded 94
      Commentary 94
      Discussion Question 95

16. Bee 96
Milk, Blood, and Excretion 96
Bee 96
Commentary 96
Discussion Questions 96
Things Other Than God 96
Discussion Question 97
Two gods? 97
Commentary 97
Discussion Question 98
Ethical Behavior 98
Discussion Questions 98

17. Beautiful Names of God 99
Doing Good 99
Discussion Question 99
Calling Evil as Good 99
Discussion Question 99
The Levels of People 99
Discussion Questions 99
Chanting and Glorification of God by All the Beings .. 100
Discussion Question 100
The Character of the Person 100
Discussion Question 100
Challenge to All Creation about the Quran 101
Discussion Questions 101
What prevents a person from believing and accepting? . 101
Discussion Questions 101
The Beautiful Names of God 102
Discussion Questions 102

18. Appreciating the Book 103
Appreciation for the Book 103
Discussion Questions 103

19. Do you hear anything from the dead? 104
Baby Jesus talks in the Cradle 104
Commentary 104
Discussion Questions 104

Contents   xi

      Do you hear anything from the dead? *104*
          Discussion Question 104
20. **Is the Quran for difficulty?** **105**
      Taha *105*
          Discussion Questions 105
21. **The Manual of a Person**. **106**
      The Manual of a Person *106*
          Discussion Question 106
22. **Creation Process**. **107**
      Creation Process. *107*
          Discussion Questions 108
23. **The Purpose** **109**
      Purpose. *109*
          Discussion Question 109
      Power struggle? *109*
          Commentary. 110
          Discussion Question 110
24. **Walking on Belly and Feet** **111**
      Walking on Belly and Feet. *111*
          Discussion Question 111
25. **Shadow and Change**. **112**
      Shadow and Change *112*
          Commentary. 112
          Discussion Questions 112
      Arrogance as a sign of ungratefulness or Prostration as
        a sign of respect? *112*
          Commentary. 113
          Discussion Question 113
26. **The Poets and Magicians**. **114**
      The Poets and Magicians. *114*
          Discussion Questions 114
      The Poets and Magicians. *115*
          Commentary. 115
          Discussion Questions 115

27. God from the Bird's Eye 116
God from the Bird's Eye 116
    Commentary 116
    Discussion Questions 117

28. Choice of Religion and Fear of Losing Wealth 118
Choosing a Religion and Fear of Losing the Wealth 118
    Discussion Questions 118

29. Struggle 119
Trials and Struggle 119
    Commentary 119
    Discussion Question 119
Struggle 120
    Commentary 120
    Discussion Questions 120
Experts of the Disciplines and Understanding the Quran 121
    Discussion Questions 121

30. Calmness with Your Spouse 122
Calmness with Your Spouse 122
    Discussion Question 122
Effect of Human's Mischief on Land and Sea 122
    Commentary 122
    Discussion Question 122
Cycle of Weakness and Strength in a Person's Life 123
    Discussion Question 123

31. Child Education 124
Child Education 124
    Commentary 124
    Discussion Question 124
Self-Accountability 125
    Discussion Questions 125

32. The Disputes and the Day of Judgment 126
The Disputes and the Day of Judgment 126
    Discussion Questions 126

Contents

33. Abuse of the Wife 127
    Two Things in One Heart or Two Hearts in One Person 127
        Commentary 127
        Discussion Question 127
    Differentiating the Role of Wife and Mother 127
        Commentary 127
        Discussion Questions 128

34. Truth and Attitude 129
    Truth and Attitude 129
        Commentary 129
        Discussion Questions 129

35. Evil and its Outcome 130
        Commentary 130
        Discussion Questions 130

36. Embryo and the Enemy 131
    Embryo and the Enemy 131
        Commentary 131
        Discussion Question 131

37. Removing the Misunderstandings about God 132
    Removing the Misunderstandings about God 132
        Commentary 132
        Discussion Question 132

38. Satan and His Mission 133
    Critical Thinking on the Quran 133
        Discussion Question 133
    Satan's Judgment of His Value 133
        Discussion Question 133
    Satan's Request to God 134
        Commentary 134
        Discussion Question 134

39. Opening the Chest and Heart 135
    The Chest 135
        Commentary 135
        Discussion Questions 135

True Appreciation of the Divine *136*
    Commentary 136
    Discussion Question 136

40. **Proving superiority through arguments?** **137**
    Discussion Questions 137

41. **Straight Path and Consistency** **138**
   Straight Path and Consistency *138*
    Discussion Questions 138
   Humility *138*
    Discussion Question 139
   Language of the Scripture *139*
    Discussion Question 139

42. **How God Communicates with Humans** **140**
   How God Communicates with Humans *140*
    Discussion Questions 140

43. **Angels and Speculations** **141**
   Angels and Speculations *141*
    Commentary 141
    Discussion Question 141

44. **Signs before the Earth's Termination** **142**
   Signs before the Earth's Termination *142*
    Commentary 142
    Discussion Question 142

45. **Accountability** **143**
   Accountability *143*
    Commentary 143
    Discussion Question 143

46. **The Mother, the Father, and the Child** **144**
   The Mother, the Father, and the Child *144*
    Commentary 144
    Discussion Questions 144

47 **Know That There Is No Deity except God** **145**
   Know That There Is No Deity except Allah *145*
    Discussion Questions 145

48.	**Tranquility and Calmness on the Heart** 146	
	Tranquility and Calmness on the Heart *146*	
	Discussion Question 146	
49.	**Social and Ethnic Classifications** 147	
	Social and Ethnic Classifications *147*	
	Commentary 147	
	Discussion Question 147	
50.	**Escape from Death** 148	
	Closer than Jugular Veins *148*	
	Discussion Question 148	
	The Intoxication of Death *148*	
	Discussion Question 148	
51.	**Escape to God** 149	
	Escape to God *149*	
	Commentary 149	
	Discussion Question 149	
	Benefit of Advice *149*	
	Discussion Question 149	
52.	**God as the Just and the Merciful in Accountability** 150	
	Discussion Question 151	
53.	**Following a Fantasy** 152	
	The Star *152*	
	Commentary 152	
	Discussion Question 152	
	Following a Fantasy *152*	
	Discussion Question 152	
54.	**The Easy Quran** 153	
	The Easy Quran *153*	
	Commentary 153	
	Discussion Questions 153	
55.	**Which favors of your Merciful, Nourishing, and Caring God will you deny?** 154	
	Which favors of your Lord will you deny? *154*	
	Commentary 154	
	Discussion Questions 154	

    Not Worshiping God Due to Preoccupation. *154*
        Discussion Questions 155

56. **Coordinates of Stars in the Universe.** **156**
    Drinking Pure Wine. *156*
        Commentary. 156
        Discussion Questions 156
    Coordinates of Stars in the Universe. *156*
        Commentary. 157
        Discussion Question 157

57. **Hardened Hearts and Remembrance of God.** **158**
    Hardened Hearts and Remembrance of God. *158*
        Commentary. 158
        Discussion Questions 158

58. **Secret Conversations** **159**
    Secret Conversations *159*
        Discussion Question 159

59. **Self and God** **160**
    Self and God. *160*
        Discussion Question 160

60. **Enemies Becoming Friends** **161**
    Enemies Becoming Friends *161*
        Discussion Questions 161

61. **Advising What You Don't Practice** **162**
    Advising What You Don't Practice *162*
        Discussion Question 162

62. **Run Away from Death**. **163**
        Discussion Question 163

63. **Not Worshipping God Due to Being Busy** **164**
    Not Worshipping God Due to Being Busy *164*
        Discussion Questions 164

64. **As Much as You Can** **165**
    As Much as You Can *165*
        Discussion Questions 165

Contents

- 65. **Financial Concerns in Divorce** 166
  - *Financial Concerns in Divorce* 166
    - Commentary 166
    - Discussion Question 166

- 66. **Two Model Women: Virgin Mary and the Wife of Pharaoh** 167
  - *The Wife of Pharaoh* 167
    - Commentary 167
    - Discussion Question 167
  - *Virgin Mary* 168
    - Discussion Question 168

- 67. **Birds** 169
  - *Birds* 169
    - Discussion Question 169

- 68. **Grasping with the Eyes** 170
    - Commentary 170
    - Discussion Question 170

- 69. **Very Little Thinking, Reflection, and Belief** 171
  - *Very Little* 171
    - Discussion Question 171
  - *And for Sure* 171
    - Discussion Questions 172

- 70. **Elevators and Paths** 173
  - *Elevators and Paths* 173
    - Commentary 173
    - Discussion Question 173

- 71. **My House** 174
  - *My House* 174
    - Commentary 174
    - Discussion Questions 174

- 72. **The unseen beings and the humans, dare to lie against God?** .. 175
  - *The unseen beings and the humans, dare to lie against God?* 175
    - Discussion Questions 175

73.	**Importance of Nights Compared to Daytime** 176	
	Importance of Nights Compared to Daytime...................... 176	
	Commentary.. 176	
	Discussion Question 176	
74.	**Clean Dress, Clean Body, and Clean Heart** 177	
	Clean Dress, Clean Body, and Clean Heart 177	
	Discussion Question 177	
75.	**Fingerprints** 178	
	Fingerprints 178	
	Commentary.. 178	
	Discussion Question 178	
	Self-Awareness 178	
	Discussion Question 178	
76.	**The Human Being** 179	
	The Human Being 179	
	Discussion Questions 179	
77.	**Embarrassment, Humiliation, and Denying the Truth** 180	
	Embarrassment, Humiliation, and Denying the Truth............... 180	
	Commentary.. 180	
	Discussion Question 180	
	Which word after this Quran? 181	
	Discussion Question 181	
78.	**The Great Event** 182	
	The Great Event 182	
	Commentary.. 182	
	Discussion Question 182	
79.	**Extractors** 183	
	(Soul) Extractors 183	
	Discussion Question 183	
80.	**Preference in Teaching** 184	
	Discussion Question 184	
81.	**Wrapping up the Sun** 185	
	Wrapping up the Sun 185	
	Discussion Question 185	

82.	Deception	186
	Deception	*186*
	Discussion Questions	186
83.	Cheating	187
	Discussion Question	187
84.	Earth, Sky, and Their Relationship with God	188
	Earth and Sky and Their Relationship with God	*188*
	Discussion Question	188
85.	Love of God	189
	Love of God	*189*
	Discussion Question	189
86.	Human Embryo Fertilization and Implantation	190
	Human Fertilization and Implantation	*190*
	Discussion Questions	190
87.	Success and Purification of the Heart	191
	Success and Purification of the Heart	*191*
	Discussion Questions	191
88.	Reminder	192
	Discussion Questions	192
89.	The Happy Self	193
	The Satisfied and Happy Self	*193*
	Commentary	193
	Discussion Question	193
90.	Two Eyes, Two Ears, and One Tongue	194
	Two Eyes, Two Ears, and One Tongue	*194*
	Discussion Question	194
91.	Success and Failure of the Self	195
	Success and Failure of the Self	*195*
	Discussion Question	195
	Right of an Animal	*196*
	Commentary	196
	Discussion Questions	196

92. The Night	**197**
The Night	197
Discussion Questions	197
93. What Is after Will Be Better	**198**
What Is after Will Be Better	198
Discussion Questions	199
94. Open Chest	**200**
Open Chest	200
Commentary	201
Discussion Questions	201
95. Perfection in Human's Creation	**202**
Perfection in Human's Creation	202
Commentary	202
Discussion Question	202
96. Read, think, and learn!	**203**
Read, think, and learn!	203
Commentary	203
Discussion Questions	203
97. The Night of Power	**204**
The Night of Power	204
Commentary	204
Discussion Questions	204
98. What is the correct and true religion for Christians and Jews?	**205**
What is the correct and true religion for Christians and Jews?	205
Discussion Questions	205
99. Atom's Weight of Good or Evil	**206**
Atom's Weight of Good or Evil	206
Discussion Question	206
100. Self-Witnessing the Ungratefulness	**207**
Self-Witnessing the Ungratefulness	207
Discussion Question	207
101. Mercy and Justice of God	**208**
Discussion Question	208

Contents

102. Knowing with Certainty 209
    Discussion Questions 209

103. Importance of Time 210
    Importance of Time 210
    Discussion Questions 210

104. Slanderer and the Mean Person 211
    Slanderer and the Mean Person 211
    Discussion Question 211

105. Holy Sites and Invalidation of the Evil Plans by God ... 212
    Discussion Questions 212

106. Holy Sites and Safety 213
    Holy Sites and Safety 213
    Discussion Questions 213

107. Being Mindful in Chants and Prayers 214
    Being Mindful in Chants and Prayers 214
    Discussion Questions 214

108. The River and Expiration 215
    Discussion Questions 215

109. Dialogue, Tolerance, and Acceptance 216
    Dialogue, Tolerance, Acceptance 216
        Commentary 216
        Discussion Question 216

110. Victory and Humbleness 217
    Victory and Humbleness 217
        Commentary 217
        Discussion Question 217

111. Evil Plots 218
    Plotting and Evil 218
        Commentary 218
        Discussion Questions 218

112. Who is God? 219
    Chapter of Sincerity and Unity 219
        Commentary 219
        Discussion Questions 220

113. Day 221
    Day *221*
        Discussion Questions 221

114. Full Protection 222
    Full Protection *222*
        Discussion Questions 222

Part 3: Preferred Translation Methodology of the Quran 223

Appendix: Perils of Translation: Text and Behavior "A Common Word among Us" in the Quran [3:64] 225
    Preferred Methodology of Translation *226*
    Introduction *226*
    Translation Theories and the Quran *227*
    Common Word *229*
    Previous Translations and Their Glitches. *231*
    Quranic Pragmatic Strategy *233*
    Review and Analysis of the Exegetical Meanings *236*
    The Core: Kalimah—A Word *239*
    Possibilities in Genres Reflected in Translations *244*
    Concluding Remarks for the Preferred Methodology of Translation *253*

Bibliography 255

Glossary 259

Acknowledgments 269

About the Author 270

Index 271

PREFACE

The first part of this book is a brief introduction to Islam with questions and answers. The second part presents selected verses from each chapter of the Quran translated to English with their interpretive contextual meanings. The third part discusses methodology of the translation used in this book as the preferred methodology of translation of the Quran from the original language of revelation, Arabic to the present-day English. This part focuses on a case study of one verse and how this can be reflected in translation as a methodology.

In this book, the relevant verses of the Quran are selected for the relevant and social contexts especially for Western readers. Muslim readers can benefit from this book by engaging different possibilities of discussion compared to their traditional education about the Quran.

The translations try to reflect the contemporary words rather than the traditional and archaic styles. The poetic style of the Quran is one of the difficult parts to reflect in the translation although there were some efforts in this book for some of the verses. To allude to this effort in this text, the color code with symmetry and rhythms are present.

Combining these three perspectives, this book can open different viewpoints especially for college readers and general readers with discussion questions.

Lastly, there are 114 chapters in the Quran. A thematic content of the selected verse is carried to the title with its original chapter number. One should not confuse this title with the normative accepted chapter names of the Quran as also presented later in this book. At least one verse is selected from each chapter of the Quran from 114 chapters. The section numbers denote the number of chapters. For verse selection of each chapter, the two numbers in brackets denote the chapter and verse numbers respectively.

Some chapters have more than one theme selection. There are more verses that could be selected from each chapter. The goal of this book is to introduce the college students and general readers to the scripture of Muslims with some selected verses.

It is a common practice that instructors select different verses of the Quran when teaching Islam. In this perspective, this valuable book makes it easy for college professors, instructors, and general readers to have an introduction to the scripture of Muslims, especially for the audience of unfamiliar readers.

Yunus Kumek, PhD
Postdoctoral Fellow
Harvard Divinity School
Spring 2018

PART 1
INTRODUCTION TO ISLAM WITH QUESTIONS AND ANSWERS

Why do we need to know about Islam?

Islam is the fastest growing and the second largest religion in the world. The number of its followers was approaching two billion in 2015. Islam is also the fastest growing religion in the United States and Europe.[1] We see and interact with Muslims daily in our lives and watch news every day related to them. There is an increasing demand in the job market, which would entail an understanding of the Muslim culture.

How was Islam started?

According to Muslim faith, Islam is not a new religion but the continuation of the original message of Abraham, Moses, Jesus, and other prophets and messengers of God, Allah. The creed, main message, of Islam is worshipping one God alone and not involving any associates with God implicitly or explicitly. In other words, Islam came to Muhammad in Arabia in 610 CE just to revive and reinstate the original message sent to Jesus, Moses, Abraham, and other messengers.

Who is Allah?

The main tenet of Islam is the belief in <u>One Creator</u>. In Islam, Allah is the proper name of the Creator among many other names and attributes of God, but the same God for Christianity and Judaism. There is no separate deity. Whether the Creator is referred to as God in English, or as YHWH in Judaism, or as Allah in Islam, it does not matter. The Creator is one. A person has a name to identify him or herself just as the Creator may have different names, but the proper name of the Creator in Islam is "Allah." The word Allah does not have either a plural form or different gender nouns. Allah is neither "he," "she," nor "it." Because of the limitations of language, "He" is the pronoun used when referring to the noun "Allah" in English although there is no humanly gender association. In the languages without gender pronouns, these pronouns are used to refer to God to minimize the issues due to anthropomorphism. Islamic scholars of philosophy[1] historically wrote

---

1. Science of kalam.

in various discourses the logical necessity of existence of the Creator, and the logical deduction of the oneness of God and perfection in God's attributes.[2]

Different Names (Attributes) of Allah, God

The Quran suggests that anyone can call God by any beautiful name,

> Say: "Call upon as Allah, God, or call upon as the Most Merciful: by whatever name you call, to God belongs the Most Beautiful Names...." [17:110]

A few of the names or attributes of God mentioned in the Quran are: the All Merciful,[2] the Very Compassionate and Merciful,[3] the Knower of All,[4] and the Just.[5] Some of these names are presented on the following page.

In Islam, the different names and means of addressing the Creator are not as important as the recognition and realization of the presence of only one Creator. After the initial belief of Oneness and Uniqueness of the Creator, it is expected for one to learn and practice the beliefs, rituals, and humane dealings to ensure that the Creator will be pleased according to the Islamic rationality.

Whenever the name of Allah is recited or uttered, Muslims add the phrase of respect next to the proper name of the Creator. For example, Allah, Jalla Jalaluhu (JJ) which means the Most High, or Subhanahu Wa Ta'ala (SWT) which means God is the Exalted One who is far from all deficiencies.

Muslims believe in one Creator. God is the same Creator who sent revelations at different times to different prophets and messengers, such as the *Torah* (Old Testament) to Moses and *the Gospel* (injil) to Jesus. In Islamic creed, creation encompasses everyone—animals, trees, stones, skies, planets, stars, microscopic viruses, and everything other than the

---

2. Ar-Rahman.
3. Ar-Rahem.
4. Al-Alim.
5. Al-Adl.

AL ASMAUL HUSNA
99 NAMES OF GOD IN ISLAM

99 BEAUTIFUL NAMES OF GOD IN ISLAM

	ALLAH	The Greatest Name
1.	Ar-Rahman	The All-Compassionate
2.	Ar-Rahim	The All-Merciful
3.	Al-Malik	The Absolute Ruler
4.	Al-Quddus	The Pure One
5.	As-Salam	The Source of Peace
6.	Al-Mu'min	The Inspirer of Faith
7.	Al-Muhaymin	The Guardian
8.	Al-'Aziz	The Victorious
9.	Al-Jabbar	The Compeller
10.	Al-Mutakabbir	The Greatest
11.	Al-Khaliq	The Creator
12.	Al-Bari'	The Maker of Order
13.	Al-Musawwir	The Shaper of Beauty
14.	Al-Ghaffar	The Forgiving
15.	Al-Qahhar	The Subduer
16.	Al-Wahhab	The Giver of All
17.	Ar-Razzaq	The Sustainer
18.	Al-Fattah	The Opener
19.	Al-'Alim	The Knower of All
20.	Al-Qabid	The Constrictor
21.	Al-Basit	The Reliever
22.	Al-Khafid	The Abaser
23.	Ar-Rafi'	The Exalter
24.	Al-Mu'izz	The Bestower of Honors
25.	Al-Mudhill	The Humiliator
26.	As-Sami	The Hearer of All
27.	Al-Basir	The Seer of All
28.	Al-Hakam	The Judge
29.	Al-'Adl	The Just
30.	Al-Latif	The Subtle One
31.	Al-Khabir	The All-Aware
32.	Al-Halim	The Forbearing
33.	Al-'Azim	The Magnificent
34.	Al-Ghafur	The Forgiver and Hider of Faults
35.	Ash-Shakur	The Rewarder of Thankfulness
36.	Al-'Ali	The Highest
37.	Al-Kabir	The Greatest
38.	Al-Hafiz	The Preserver
39.	Al-Muqit	The Nourisher
40.	Al-Hasib	The Accounter
41.	Al-Jalil	The Mighty
42.	Al-Karim	The Generous
43.	Ar-Raqib	The Watchful One
44.	Al-Mujib	The Responder to Prayer
45.	Al-Wasi'	The All-Comprehending
46.	Al-Hakim	The Perfectly Wise
47.	Al-Wadud	The Loving One
48.	Al-Majid	The Majestic One
49.	Al-Ba'ith	The Resurrector
50.	Ash-Shahid	The Witness
51.	Al-Haqq	The Truth
52.	Al-Wakil	The Trustee
53.	Al-Qawi	The Possessor of All Strength
54.	Al-Matin	The Forceful One
55.	Al-Wali	The Governor
56.	Al-Hamid	The Praised One
57.	Al-Muhsi	The Appraiser
58.	Al-Mubdi	The Originator
59.	Al-Mu'id	The Restorer
60.	Al-Muhyi	The Giver of Life
61.	Al-Mumit	The Taker of Life
62.	Al-Hayy	The Ever Living One
63.	Al-Qayyum	The Self-Existing One
64.	Al-Wajid	The Finder
65.	Al-Majid	The Glorious
66.	Al-Wahid	The One
67.	Al-Ahad	The One and Only
68.	As-Samad	The Satisfier of All Needs
69.	Al-Qadir	The All Powerful
70.	Al-Muqtadir	The Creator of All Power
71.	Al-Muqaddim	The Expediter
72.	Al-Mu'akhkhir	The Delayer
73.	Al-Awwal	The First
74.	Al-Akhir	The Last
75.	Az-Zahir	The Manifest One
76.	Al-Batin	The Hidden One
77.	Al-Wali	The Protecting Friend
78.	Al-Muta'ali	The Supreme One
79.	Al-Barr	The Doer of Good
80.	At-Tawwab	The Guide to Repentance
81.	Al-Muntaqim	The Avenger
82.	Al-Afu	The Forgiver
83.	Ar-Ra'uf	The Clement
84.	Malik al-Mulk	The Owner of All
85.	Dhul-Jalali Wal-Ikram	The Lord of Majesty and Bounty
86.	Al-Muqsit	The Equitable One
87.	Al-Jami	The Gatherer
88.	Al-Ghani	The Rich One
89.	Al-Mughni	The Enricher
90.	Al-Mani'	The Preventer of Harm
91.	Ad-Darr	The Creator of The Harmful
92.	An-Nafi	The Creator of Good
93.	An-Nur	The Light
94.	Al-Hadi	The Guide
95.	Al-Badi	The Originator
96.	Al-Baqi	The Everlasting One
97.	Al-Warith	The Inheritor of All
98.	Ar-Rashid	The Righteous Teacher
99.	As-Sabur	The Patient One

Different Names (Attributes) of Allah, God

© Africa Studio/Shutterstock.com

Creator. Allah is the Creator. God is One. God is Unique in the Divine Attributes. God does not resemble any of the creation. God does not have a father or a mother. God does not give birth. God does not need anything because need indicates dependence and that is a defect for the Creator. On the other hand, all the created, everything and everyone, needs God. The created can only understand God through the Divine Attributes. God's attributes are described in the Holy Quran and in the Hadith, the sayings of the Prophet Muhammad. The words "hadith" or "sunnah" can refer to the statements and actions of the Prophet Muhammad as well as the conditions that were approved by him in his lifetime.

Several chapters and verses in the Quran describe the attributes of God. One of the famous chapters is the chapter of Ikhlas (Sincerity).

Arabic to English Transliteration of Chapter of Ikhlas (Sincerity):

Bismillah ir-Rahman ir-Raheem

1. Qul huwa Allahu Ahad
2. Allahu 's-Samad
3. Lam yalid wa lam yulad
4. Wa lam yakul lahu kufuwan Ahad

English Translation of Verses of Chapter of Ikhlas (Sincerity):

1. English Translation by Muhammad Shameem, Mohammad Wali Raazi, and Muhammad Taqi Usmani[3]:

Say, "The truth is: Allah is One. Allah is Besought of all, needing none. [He neither begot anyone, nor was He begotten. And has never any one been equal to Him."]

2. English Translation by Mohammed Marmaduke Pickthall[4]:

Say: He is Allah, the One! [Allah, the eternally Besought of all! He begets not nor is he begotten. And there is none comparable unto Him.]

3. English Translation by Yusuf Ali[5]:

Say: He is Allah, the One and Only; Allah, the Eternal, the Absolute; He begets not, nor is He begotten; And there is none comparable unto Him.

Simpler Translation and Explanation of Chapter of Ikhlas (Sincerity):

1. Oh Muhammad! Proclaim that God is One. (Another verse compels people to think that if there is more than one creator there will be chaos in the universe.)
2. God does not need anyone/anything, but everyone and everything needs God. (Need is a defect for the Creator.)
3. God does not give birth. God does not have a child or children. God does not have a father or a mother. (The Creator should not be dependent on a father or mother. God has no beginning and end according to the Islamic creed.)
4. There is nothing comparable to God.

Muslims recite this chapter all the time both during prayers as well as outside of prayers to get rewards from Allah. The reward for reading this short chapter is great because it explains the attributes of Allah.

On the other hand, it is forbidden to reflect on the essence and entity of the Creator. The creation is limited by the capacity of his mind, vision, hearing, and all other physical conditions. Therefore, the limited creation cannot grasp the Unlimited Creator. One of the established notions in Islamic creed is that understanding the Creator is gaining the understanding that the person cannot fully understand God, because the limited cannot understand the Unlimited. Understanding something means grasping or surrounding intellectually. God the Infinite cannot be, therefore, grasped with the limited creation. In the Quran, it says "The eyes cannot encompass God but God can encompass the eyes . . ." [6:103].

For many mystic Muslims the purpose of life is getting closer to Allah with worship and knowledge. This is not a physical closeness. Allah is closer to the person than him or herself but the person can be disconnected. This is sometimes referred to as knowledge of God.[6]

---
6. Ma'rufatullah in Arabic.

In this perspective, the knowledge of the Creator is essential in Islamic theology. It is understood that "the Quran's heart is beating as the oneness of the Creator." Therefore, the true understanding of God is a main focus of the Quran. Therefore, it is an orthodox teaching that any type of knowledge deprived of this will not be complete.

Who is the Prophet Muhammad?

Muhammad is the name of the last prophet in Islam. He is a human role model, selected by God to confirm the previous messages of other role model messengers such as Jesus, Moses, and Abraham. According to most Islamic scholars, the collective wisdom of humanity is constructed by all the prophets. Although there are only twenty-five prophets mentioned in the Quran, one narration from Prophet Muhammad states that God sent more than 124,000 prophets at different times to different groups of people since the beginning of the human history.[6] Because God is merciful and caring, God would not leave humans without any guidance and purpose on earth. Some Islamic scholars suggest that Buddha and Confucius could be prophets of God but that the followers of these great men changed their original teachings over time.[7]

The Prophet Muhammad received prophethood at the age of forty. Compared to his peers, he had a distinctive life before he attained prophethood. Some of his traits before prophethood were:

- He did not worship idols, which was a major religious rite in his society.
- He recognized the One and Only Creator.
- He was known by his peers in his society for his ethical and virtuous traits.
- He was respected, and consulted in decision-making due to his trustworthiness.
- He was given responsibilities to protect women, orphans, and community valuables, due to his trustworthiness.
- He opposed certain practices of his society such as female infanticide, usury, and tribal wars due to blood vengeance.

- He performed spiritual retreats before his prophethood. In his spiritual retreats, he contemplated and was concerned about unethical practices of his society.

One can refer to other books[8][9] on the detailed traits and character of the Prophet Muhammad. After receiving revelation from God at the age of forty, he became the messenger of God, living among people and teaching the verses of the Quran as it was revealed to him in his remaining life of twenty-three years. An example of a verse from the Quran that Prophet Muhammad is required to disclose what has been revealed to him is as follows [5:67]:

> O Messenger, announce that which has been revealed to you from your God, and if you do not, then you have not conveyed God's message. And Allah will protect you from the people. Indeed, Allah does not guide the people of unappreciators and unrecognizers of God.

In other words, the Prophet Muhammad is instructed not to hide even a little portion from the revelation. If this was not the case, then his true prophethood would have been challenged. In the above verse, God is giving assurance that the Prophet will be under the protection of God. After the revelation of the verse [5:67], the Prophet avoided use of any personal protection measure (such as use of escorts or bodyguards) despite the fact that there were several assassination attempts on his life through physical attack, poisoning, or black magic[10][11] as mentioned in different sources of Islamic history and hadith.

The humanness of the Prophet Muhammad is frequently underlined and emphasized in Islam. Although the Prophet Muhammad is the main teacher and messenger in Islam and venerated exceptionally, he is a creation, human, and worshipper of God. This notion itself is much emphasized in the Quran and in the sayings of the Prophet Muhammad as well. The reason for this is to prevent any type of idolatry through disproportionate veneration except worshipping One God alone. According to the Islamic history, most of the idols were either prophets or saints of God in different times and had become idols due to disproportionate veneration.[12] Therefore, this teaching prevails repeatedly in Islamic system of creed. In the Quran,

Say [O Prophet]: I am but a mortal man like all of you. However, it has been revealed unto me that your God is the One and Only God. Hence, whoever looks forward [with hope and awe] to meeting his Sustainer [on Judgment Day], let him do righteous deeds, and let him not ascribe unto anyone or anything a share in the worship due to his Sustainer!" [18:110].[13]

Say thou, [O Prophet:] "I am but a mortal like you. It has been revealed to me that your God is the One God: go, then, straight towards to God and seek God's forgiveness!" And woe unto those who ascribe divinity besides God [41:6].[13]

The upcoming section also shows examples of Prophet Muhammad's miracles which are extraordinary and unusual occurrences through God's empowerment to affirm his prophethood.

According to the hadith scholars, it was imperative to preserve even the smallest details about the life of the Prophet for the benefit of upcoming generations. Therefore, one can find narrations from the Prophet's companions about the length of the Prophet's eyelashes, the quantity of his hair, how his skin felt when touched, his body posture while walking, etc.[7]

What is the Quran?

The Quran is the name of the sacred text of Muslims. The Quran is a sacred book confirming and protecting the messages of the Bible: the Gospel, the Psalms, and the Torah.

Over a period of twenty-three years, the Quran was revealed by God to Prophet Muhammed through the angel Gabriel. There are verses in the Quran that describe the book as the light and guidance for those who desire to lift themselves from the abyss of spiritual darkness and oppression into divine light and freedom. Also, there are verses in the Quran that describe how the holy book is to be read and benefited from. It strongly advises that it should be read with reflection and thinking.[7] While one is reading the Quran during and outside prayers, it is the

---

7. Tadabbur in Ar.

traditional practice of the Prophet Muhammad and Muslims that they engage themselves with the text as an interactive interface. For example, when a person is reading the verses related to reward and Heaven, a person may beseech God to be included among the dwellers of Heaven. On the contrary, while reading the verses of punishment, a person may seek God's protection from it. When a person is reading the verses related to the applications of moral behavior, one can seek God's help to be just and ethical in one's position of authority.[11]

According to the Quranic verses, the Quran was revealed by God not to oppose the Bible: the Gospel, the Psalms, and the Torah but it came to confirm them. The second quality of the Quran is to protect the authenticity of the Bible: the Gospel, the Psalms, and the Torah. This is mentioned in the below verse of the Quran:

> Then We revealed the Book to you (O Muhammad!) with Truth, confirming whatever of the Book was revealed before, and protecting and guarding over it. [5:48]

There are numerous verses in the Quran referring to Bible: the Gospel, the Psalms, and the Torah. In these verses of the Quran, God mentions the sameness of the message that was revealed in all these sacred texts about worshipping only One God and not associating open or secret partnership with God.

The preparation for the afterlife, and the existence of rewards and punishment, are other important and frequent topics that are discussed in the Quran. The Quran critiques the dealings of the clergy of the previous books, such as the Bible: the Gospel, the Psalms, and the Torah, in their attempts to change the original teachings of the revelation from God. In numerous verses in the Quran, this is described as "selling the verses of God for a cheap worldly price." According to the Quran, one of the major examples of the alteration of the authenticity of the previous sacred texts is about the verses related to the correct understanding of God.

The Quran strongly condemns defaming and insulting narratives of other prophets and messengers in the Bible: the Gospel, the Psalms, and the Torah. According to Islamic scholarship, some of these narratives are also considered to be the altered portions of these divine scriptures.[14]

Alternatively, one can find the narratives of the Virgin Mary, Moses, Abraham, Lot, and Jesus repetitively in the Quran with similar and different contextual meanings. One can notice a lot of similarities and differences with the Bible: the Gospel, the Psalms, and the Torah in certain perspectives. The differences of the prophetic narratives of the Quran compared to the narratives in the Bible: the Gospel, the Psalms, and the Torah are mostly about the ethical and pious stances of the prophets as role models.

On the other hand, in other instances, the Quran applauds the sincerity of some of the Christians who reflect on the verses of God in the universe, and take lessons from them in awe, respect, and fear. The Quran approves the ethical stance of Jews in different times supporting the good and preventing evil. In all cases of the narratives of the previous nations following Christianity and Judaism, they are presented as the true believers of their time. Their virtues and mistakes are mentioned in the Quran for readers in order to take a lesson from it but not to form isolated social and religious groups. Below is a piece from Carl Ernst's book of *How to read the Quran*:

> While the Quran overlaps with the Bible on certain subjects, it is unfamiliar enough in its distinctive narratives and in its stylistic peculiarities that many first-time readers have pronounced it to be impenetrable. The strangeness of the Quran for the Jewish and Christian reader lies in the fact that it does not repeat earlier biblical texts but instead makes brief allusions to them while providing a new and original synthesis that departs from familiar ways of reading the Old and New Testaments. (p. 4.)[15]

The Quran does not establish a mere group identity based on cultural inheritance of religion. Rather, it encompasses all the religions, especially Judaism, Christianity, and Islam, and critiques and constructs a pure, natural, but at the same time, logical way of belief and lifestyle for humanity. An unfamiliar reader of the Quran can be mistaken if the verses are taken out of their cultural, historical, and reason based contexts. This problem can be true for any type of literal or out of context readings for any religious or non-religious books. Therefore, it is important to analyze the Quran as one whole piece in accordance with interpretations of the Prophet Muhammad as found in the traditions or hadith.

There are different opinions why the Quran is a miracle. It is a miracle because of its prophecies about scientific and social events. According to some, the Quran was revealed with a very unique style, especially when the Arab poetry and literature was at its zenith. There have been people who became Muslim after being exposed to the Quranic verses since the beginning of the revelation. Some contemporary scholars argue that the Quran never gets old, although human texts tend to lose their attraction over time. The Quran has always been compatible with scientific discoveries, and for the solutions of the social and individual problems according to Islamic scholars.[16] One of the interesting perspectives noted by the contemporary scholars[17] is that the Quran uses different languages in different instances. For example, when it is talking about a person's spiritual and evil problems, a physician's language is used instead of engineering language. The interpretation is that humans are complicated. It takes time to get sick and it takes time to heal. It is not like engineering where one can find the problem and fix it immediately. The cases of hypocrisy, denial, unappreciative behavior, self-conceit, arrogance, oppression, abuse, hate, and aggression are some of the diseases mentioned in the Quran. One can, for example, find the methodology of pathology in social diseases when observing the issues of moral philosophy.

Authenticity of the Quran

Over a period of twenty-three years, the Quran was revealed by God to Prophet Muhammed in Arabic language. As the verses were being revealed from Allah, God, the Prophet had special individuals[8] assigned for writing the revelation while the Prophet was alive. Besides this, as the revelation continued, the general public: the companions and friends[9] of

---

8. Referred to as the revelation writers.
9. Sahabah in Ar.

the Prophet Muhammad both memorized the verses and wrote them on different types of writing materials. The primary motivation of writing and memorization of the verses for the early Muslims was to recite the revealed verses in their own prayers. In a Muslim daily prayer,[10] a person should recite the Quranic verses from memory. This practice made thousands of followers memorize the entire Quran. Although writing and recording the Quran did exist during the time of the Prophet, one of the main ways of preserving the Quran has been through the tradition of memorization. In the education of this oral tradition, as the Islamic governments were established, it has become a tradition to open specialized memorization schools[11] of the Quran.[12] In this method of preservation of the Quran, Muslims have been meticulous even pronouncing one letter of the Quran correctly in its flawless recitation. This science is referred to as the correct recitation of the Quran, tajweed. To give an example, if a person attends a Muslim prayer in a mosque or in any place, praying in a congregation, it is better and more rewarding than praying alone according to the teachings of the Prophet. To implement this teaching, a person stands in the front to lead the prayer.[13] This person loudly reads the Quranic verses from memory and the people behind listen to him. If this person makes a mistake in recitation of the Quran, then one can observe and hear that the followers are correcting the lead person. This tradition has been practiced since the beginning of Islam in both Arab and non-Arab cultures.

It is required to recite the Quran in Arabic because the Quran was revealed in the Arabic language. Any translation is considered as the interpretation although the meanings can be close. Therefore, one can find lengthy titles such as "the translation of the meaning of the Quran with interpretive meanings" in the translated versions of the Quran. The purpose is to simply tell the reader that what the person is reading is not the authentic and original Quran but approximated meanings in that language of translation. The original and authentic sacred text, the Quran, is in Arabic, not in any other language. This emphasis is also

---

10. Referred to as Salah in Arabic speaking cultures and namaz in Indian, Persian, and Turkish cultures.
11. Sometimes called madrasa.
12. This is known as "Hifz" in Arabic. Hafiz is the honarary title given to the person who memorized the entire Quran.
13. Referred to as Imam.

made in various verses of the Quran itself that the Quran is in Arabic, not in any other language.

This does not mean that a non-Arab should not read the Quran. It is encouraged to read the translations with explanatory notes to give the context and intended meanings rather than looking merely on the simple and possibly incorrect misleading literal meanings of the words in the translated language. This is true even for Arab readers as well because knowing the rules of the proper language and knowing the Quranic sciences needs a separate training and education.

What do Muslims believe?

Six Articles of Faith in Islam

Iman is generally translated as the Islamic belief system. A person who has iman is called a believer (mu'min) in Islam. Islamic faith (iman) is based on six parts. These six parts include believing in

- ▶ The Creator (Allah)
- ▶ The Books
- ▶ The Prophets
- ▶ The Angels
- ▶ The Afterlife
- ▶ The Destiny

In Islamic terminology, belief is a dual process that requires believing from the heart as well as advocating that belief is through speech, that is, by speaking using the tongue. The tongue and the heart are, therefore, the two complimentary physical organs that satisfy the needs of Islamic faith.

Who is God for Muslims?

The Belief in the Creator

In Islamic terminology, the explanation of the concept of the unity of God or the Creator is referred to as tawhid. Tawhid might be translated as Islamic monotheism. The opposite of tawhid is shirk, which could be referred to as polytheism. In Islam, the branch of the science that explains tawhid is called "kalam" or "aqaid." One of the famous scholars of this science is Imam Tahawi. He explains the core principles of tawhid very concisely in his book called *Aqaid Tahawiyah*.[18] Below is my rendering of the partial translation from his work.

God: The Divine and the Creator

God is One, without any partners. There is nothing like God. There is nothing that can overwhelm God. There is no god other than God. God is the Eternal without a beginning and enduring without end. God will never perish nor come to an end. No imagination can fully conceive God and no understanding can fully comprehend God. God is different from any created being. God is living and never dies and is eternally active and never sleeps. God creates without being in need to do so and provides for the creation without any effort. God causes death with no fear and restores to life without difficulty. God has always existed together with the eternal attributes since before creation. Bringing creation into existence did not add anything to God's attributes that were not already there. As God was, together with the attributes, in pre-eternity, so God will remain throughout endless time. It was not only after the act of creation that God could be described as "the Creator," nor was it only by the act of origination that God could be described as "the Originator."

God was always the Lord even when there was nothing to be Lord of, and always the Creator even when there was no creation. God is exalted beyond having opposites or equals. Anyone who describes God as being in any way the same as a human is not a believer. All those who grasp this will take heed and refrain from saying things such as the unbelievers say, and they will know that God, in the attributes, is not like human beings. God is beyond having limits placed on God, or being restricted, or having parts or limbs. Nor is God contained by the six directions as all created things are. God encompasses all things and what God has created is incapable of encompassing God. God has absolute control over everything and nothing has any control over God. Nothing can be independent of God even for the blinking of an eye, and whoever considers herself or himself independent of God for the blinking of an eye is guilty of unbelief.[18]

Why is belief in one God the core of Islam?

Three of the major sins in Islam are not believing in one Creator, transgressing the rights of parents, and killing someone as narrated by the Prophet.[19] According to some scholars, these three cases are all related. A child who does not recognize and appreciate the right of a mother and father is considered in the state of a major denial of the favors of the parents. These favors could be a mother going through hardship of carrying her child for nine months in the state of sickness and pains of labor and delivery, breastfeeding after birth, and physical and spiritual upbringing of the child by both mother and the father. This unappreciative state of the child could be due to arrogance or denial, despite being aware of all these favors. In a similar way, according to Islamic creed, Allah gives a very minute role to the parents about upbringing a child compared to the Divine role but expects an immense appreciation to the favors of the parents. By doing this, this may lead a person either to go to Heaven or it may harshly cause the person to go for a just accountability. In other words, according to Islam, God (Allah) deserves more appreciation and recognition about the Divine favors than parents. In reality, God is the one who gives life in a mother's womb, giving sustenance, strength, and all the ecological and social environment for a person to exist. The Divine expectation is that the person knows, accepts, and appreciates that there is a Creator who has given all these bounties to the person. The person appreciates it firstly by believing in the One and only Creator, then he or she could be called in a state of appreciation called a believer or a Muslim. Then, as a believer, finding ways to please God through the ways of the prophets such as Muhammad who represents in his prophetic teachings the paths of the previous messengers, and prophets such as Jesus, Moses, David, Abraham, and so forth. The roles of the prophets are all complimentary to each other and they are not in the state of competing and conflicting with each other.

How do Muslims understand miracles?

Miracles

In Islamic belief, prophets and messengers of God are empowered to show miracles to prove that their message is the truth. In other words, the main purpose of a miracle is to prove the truthfulness and sincerity of the apostle. Showing miracles is only one vehicle for the authenticity of the true messengership or prophethood. Miracles[14] occur only with the help of God's power[15] and knowledge.[16] If any prophet or messenger or apostle performs a miracle, it is the Creator (Allah) who gives them that empowerment to do so.

The Quran mentions several miracles in relation to the Prophets Abraham, Moses, Jesus, and many others. For example, the Quran mentions the miracle of a blazing bonfire that failed to hurt Abraham, the burning bush encounter of Moses, and the miraculous birth of Jesus by the Virgin Mary without any sexual encounter.

According to the Islamic doctrine, the supreme miracle of the Prophet Muhammad is the Quran itself because it is still unchanged, authentic, and it is still alive with people. The Quran has in itself convoluted miracles, miracles within miracles, related to prophecies, scientific discoveries, therapeutic effects, language, literature, rationality, and philosophy according to many exegetical scholars.[16] This scripture, the Quran, was revealed to a person, Muhammad, who was neither a complex intellectual nor a revered philosopher. Rather, he was an unsophisticated, pure, innocent, genuine and sincere person, who prior to his prophethood was regarded as a model of high moral and ethical standards in his society. The Prophet Muhammad performed various miracles. Amongst others, some of these miracles include curing the sick, conversing with stones, splitting of the moon, gushing of water from his fingers at a time of drought and having thousands of people quenching their thirst with this water, etc. However, his enduring legacy as a miracle is considered to be the Quran, an opinion unanimously agreed on by Islamic scholars.[20]

---

14. Mu'jizah in Ar.
15. Qudrah in Ar.
16. I'lm in Ar.

Who is a prophet or messenger in Islam?

Believing in Prophets

Muslims are required to believe in all true messengers and prophets sent by God at different times with varying missions. In Islam, it is required to believe in Jesus, Moses, Abraham, and all others sent by God. Therefore, if a Muslim makes a statement that "I believe in Muhammad but I don't believe in Jesus," then according to the Islamic canonized creed system, this person is not a Muslim.[18]

The understanding of prophets or messengers sent by God is somehow similar and different than the Judeo-Christian tradition. In Islamic narratives and understanding, the prophets have certain attributes. They are role models, truthful, trusted, insightful, and infallible.[21] Infallibility is not because they are like angels. They have the choice and free will of either doing evil or good, but with God's mercy and protection, they always choose to do good. In other words, they use their free will in decision-making to choose correctly and ethically. Therefore, one can find the Quranic and Biblical narratives about a messenger or a prophet of God to be similar in some aspects and yet divergent in others. The primary divergence point is the content of the Quranic narratives due to the infallibility and truthfulness of these messengers. According to different discourses,[22] it is not logical that God would send them as exemplary individuals and yet these prophets will act otherwise. Therefore, the prophets in Islam are sent by God as the role models to show that God's commands are practical and possible to implement as humans. One of the attributes of the prophets and messengers of God is that they call people to the ethical and moral ways, and also steer people towards the true recognition and appreciation of One Creator. One can find very similar narratives about prophets such as Abraham, Jonah, Noah, and Moses in the Quran and the previous divine scriptures (Bible: the Gospel, the Psalms, and the Torah). One can even find similarities in the names of different prophets, messengers, and other important people in Islam and Judeo-Christian tradition which may be surprising for the unfamiliar reader. Some of these are presented below:

Name in Judeo-Christian Tradition	Name in Islam
Abraham	Ibrahim
Moses	Musa
David	Dawud
Solomon	Sulayman
Zechariah	Zakariya
Jesus	Isa
Noah	Nuh

It is interesting to note that Muslims refer to Jesus as "Jesus Christ." In other words, Muslims are required to believe in Jesus as the Christ due to teachings of the Quran and the Prophet Muhammad. Similarly, just like the Christians, Muslims revere John the Baptist. In accordance to the teachings of the Quran and the Prophet Muhammad, Muslims are required to believe that John was baptized. The Arabic name for the Virgin Mary is Maryam, the mother of Jesus.

Muslims believe that Allah created all the community of beings with a purpose, with a guide or a leader. Allah gave bees a queen, ants a leader, and birds and fish each a guide, and a prophet for human beings to guide them to a spiritual, intellectual, and material perfection. Although it may be possible for some people to find the Creator by reflecting upon nature, but human beings still need a prophet or a messenger from God to learn why they were created, where they came from, where they are going, and how to worship the Creator properly. Islam teaches that God sent prophets to teach people the true meaning of creation, to unveil the mysteries behind historical and natural events, and to inform them of their relationship with the divine Scriptures and the universe.

Some Muslim scholars have suggested that without prophets, mankind couldn't have made significant scientific progress.[7] Throughout human history, Prophets have guided humanity in intellectual and scientific illumination. Prophet Adam pioneered farming, Prophet Enoch was known for tailoring, Prophet Noah was skilled in ship-making, and Joseph was proficient in clock making. More importantly, Prophets have taught the guidelines of social life based on justice, respect, and ethical values.

Whenever people departed from the original teachings of a prophet, God sent another one to teach them again in both belief and ethical values. This continued until the coming of the last Prophet Muhammad as mentioned in the Quran [33:40]. According to Islamic theology, prophethood and messengership ended with Prophet Muhammad but God continues to send different scholars and saints to revive the religion.

Muslims believe in all the prophets and messengers sent by God, and make no distinction among them. A verse in the Quran (my contextual and exegetical translation) says:

> The prophet believed in the Revelation
> The believers believed in the Revelation
> Everyone believed in One, and Only God
> Everyone believed in Gabriel, Michael, and all angels
> Everyone believed in the Bible: the Gospel, the Psalms, and the Torah, and Quran and all the scriptures
> Everyone believed in Moses, Jesus, Muhammad as the chosen messengers from God
> Everyone believed other messengers and all the prophets chosen by God
> There is no superiority of one book over another
> There is no superiority of one prophet over another

And they ended their proclamation as:

> We received the message and surrendered and submitted
>   Oh God
> You are Our only, One, the most Merciful God
> We will meet with You soon [2:285]

The above verse is an example of why Muslims believe that Islam is a universal and inclusive religion.

Miracles and Divinity

In Islamic belief, performing miracles by a prophet is an attestation of authenticity. God possibly sent this person and he is special. However, showing a miracle is not a sufficient indication to be a prophet of God but merely a possibility. Therefore, God empowers prophets with miracles to prove their legitimacy. The main purpose of a miracle is to prove the apostle's truthfulness and sincerity. Miracles occur only with God's permission, power, and knowledge. If any prophet, messenger, or apostle performs a miracle, it is the Creator (God) bestowing such empowerment. As mentioned in the Quran, God previously empowered the prophets and messengers such as Abraham, Moses, Jesus, and many others. The Quran does not overtly describe the Prophet Muhammad's various miracles. According to Islamic doctrine, the supreme miracle of the prophet is the Quran itself because:

- The Quran was revealed to an illiterate person, Prophet Muhammad.
- The Quran talks about unseen events and provides detailed information on past events such as stories of the past prophets, and information about the future such as the war between Byzantines and Persians.
- There is no contradiction in the Quran.
- The Quran provides authentic information on nature and creation.
- The Quran contains information about the society and relations between different groups.
- No verse of the Quran contradicts known scientific knowledge.

Some of the other miracles of Prophet Muhammad are:

- The Prophet's exemplary moral and ethical life. Until the age of 40, before Prophethood, he was already an established role model in his community with his exemplary moral and ethical life.
- The earlier scriptures such as the Bible: the Gospel, the Psalms, and the Torah, forecasting about the upcoming of the Prophet Muhammad. The Christian and Jewish scholars were already in prediction from their scriptures a new coming messenger of God at that region around the time of the Muhammad.

- Splitting the moon: When the Prophet was challenged to about the authenticity of his messengership from God, the Prophet Muhammad split the moon by pointing to it with his finger as a miracle and kept it split in the range of seconds to minutes and then brought it back to its original form with the empowerment and enablement of God. This incident was narrated by numerous witnesses in the science of authentication of hadith.
- Heavenly journey-ascension: Muslims believe Prophet Muhammad ascended unto the Heavens with the guide of the Arc Angel Gabriel. On this heavenly journey, he met with all the prior messengers (such as Adam, Noah, Abraham, Moses, and Jesus) and they all prayed together under his leadership in Jerusalem. Finally, Prophet Muhammad met with God and God bestowed him with five times daily prayer as a gift to all the believers. Then, the Prophet descended back unto earth to complete his mission among people as the messenger of God until his demise.
- Speaking of stones in his hand: When the Prophet Muhammad picked up a handful of stones from the ground, the pebbles started glorifying God as a miracle. This was witnessed by people next to him and they heard the chanting of the stones while the Prophet was holding them according to the authentic chain of narrations.
- Miracle of the talking poisoned meat: Along with his companions, the Prophet was invited to a dinner by a woman of the prior scriptures. To test and ascertain the prophet's call, the woman administered poison into the meal (cooked meat). According to authenticated narrations, the cooked meat informed the prophet of its poisonous nature and told him not to consume it.
- Feeding hundreds of people with one bowl of food: It is reported that during time of scarcity of food, the Prophet prayed on a bowl of food and then, hundreds of people ate from this bowl without the food finishing in the bowl.
- Lamentations of a wood pillar: It is also reported that when a wood pillar was being removed from the mosque, a loud cry emanated from the piece of wood. The Prophet often leaned against this pillar while in the mosque and it is believed that its expected separation from the Prophet caused it great distress.

- Conversations with animals: Some animals spoke to the Prophet and complained of the abuse they endured from their owners.

For all the incidents above, there are multiple authentic narrators and witnesses according to the Islamic tradition.[10]

In Islamic creed, the messengers perform the supernatural events or miracles with the empowerment of the Creator but not through their own ability. Therefore, the full credit is given to the Creator. The Creator (and not the messenger or the prophet) is divine. Claiming divinity for any of God's creations including the prophets is an immense sin in Islam. Therefore, Muslims believe that Jesus is one of the selected apostles of the Creator along with other prophets such as Abraham, Moses, David, Muhammad, and others. No one is divine except Allah. The Quran draws similarity between Adam and Jesus' creations. While Jesus only had no father, Adam neither had a mother nor a father. Both of their creations are considered God's miracles. The below verses allude to this notion:

> The similitude of Jesus before God is as that of Adam; God created him from dust, then said to him "Be": and he was.[5] [the Quran, 3:59]

> O People of the Book! Commit no excesses in your religion: Nor say of God aught but the truth. Jesus Christ, the son of Mary was (no more than) a Messenger of Allah, and God's Word, which God bestowed on Mary, a Spirit proceeding from God, so believe in God and God's Messengers. Say not "Trinity", desist! it will be better for you. Your Creator, is indeed One Creator, Glory be to God, far Exalted is God above having a son. To God belong all things in the heavens and on earth. And, enough is God as a Disposer of affairs. [the Quran, 4:171][5]

In another chapter in the Quran, there is a dialogue between Jesus and Allah:

> And behold! God will say: "O Jesus, the son of Mary! Did you say to human beings, 'Worship me and my mother as gods in derogation of Allah'?" He will say: "Glory to You! Never could I say what I had no right (to say). Had I said such a thing, though you would indeed have known it. You know what is in my heart,

although, I do not know what is in You. You know in full all that is hidden. [the Quran 5:116][5]

Muslim scholars interpret the above verses of the Quran as the clear indication of acceptance and declaration of Jesus that he is the created being of Allah, and Jesus was sent similar to other prophets to guide people to the teachings of God. So, Muslims believe that Jesus is an important prophet and messenger of God but not son of God.

Prophet Muhammad's tomb and Mosque in Madina, Saudi Arabia

Do the Muslims believe in the Bible: the Gospel, the Psalms, and the Torah?

Belief in the Divine Books

Muslims are required to believe in all the books that were revealed by God. In the creed system, a Muslim is required to believe in the Quran, the Bible: the Gospel, the Psalms, and the Torah and all other communications sent by God. Therefore, if a person says "I believe in the Quran but I don't believe in the Bible: the Gospel, the Psalms, and the Torah that was sent by God," then this person is not a Muslim according to the canonized teachings.[18]

However, Muslims make a distinction that they believe in the authentic versions of these sacred books. Some of these books are mentioned in the Quran. They are the the Gospel (injil), the Psalms (zabur) and the torah (tawrah), and other books or canons that were revealed to different prophets at different times such as Adam and Abraham. The Quran mentions that in all the previous books, God has stated the same message of worshiping one (and only) God. There is no change in the message but God sent at different times the same message due to the modification of the original message by the people over time as mentioned in the verses in the Quran:

> And when God took a promise from those who were given the earlier scriptures stating that "you must make it clear and explain this scripture to the people but not conceal it." But still they hid it and exchanged it for a cheap price. And what a bad and lowly deal that they did! [3:187]

> Oh followers of the earlier scriptures! there has come to you Our Messenger, Muhammad making clear to you much of what you used to conceal from the scriptures and overlooking much. There has come to you from God a light and a clear Book, the Quran. [5:15] (adapted from[23]).

Confirming Scripture or Confirming Book is another name the Quran uses for the divine revelation for itself. It is due to the understanding of the Quran as the scripture confirming the Christian Bible: the Gospel, the Psalms, and the Torah. The Quran values Christian, Jewish, and all other divine scriptures as the scriptures of God.

As stated[24]:

> The notion of the Confirming Book is one of the emphasizing notions in the theology of practice as well. In the accepted and canonized understanding of the scripture in the theology, the position of the Quran is not to compete with the Bible: the Gospel, the Psalms, and the Torah, but its position is to detail, confirm and complement the other divine books.[17] As an

---
17. Musaddiq is used in the Quran.

example: a genuine parent will not have preference among their children. He or she will expect the siblings to help each other. Similarly, the divine books in their essence stabilize each other in reaching one goal: achieving and establishing a path to the Divine.

Are the angels in Islam similar to those in Christianity and Judaism?

Belief in Angels

Although there are rational arguments by Islamic scholars about the existence of angels, it is ultimately a belief that Muslims need to submit and accept that there are unseen beings other than humans that are created by God. In this case, these are angels who are created by God. They perform actions in the physical, metaphysical, seen, and unseen worlds with the order of God. There are angels who are with each person protecting them. There are angels who record the deeds of each person. One can realize the similar beliefs in the teachings of Christianity and Judaism with Islam. Therefore, one can even find similarities among these traditions for the specific names of angels. For example:

Name of the Angel in Judeo-Christian Tradition	Name of the Angel in Islam	Angel's Duty
Gabriel	Jabrael or Jibril	Bringing revelation from God to the selected messengers and prophets
Michael	Mikaeel	Maintaining the natural laws

According to the exegetical scholars' interpretation of some verses in the Quran, "Ruhul Qudus" is one of Angel Gabriel's titles. This title can be roughly translated as "Holy spirit" in English language. Therefore, some of the Muslim scholars explain the possible confusion of Christians in the interpretation of Angel Gabriel as the part of the divinity, because this angel was bringing a message from God to the prophets. Thus, some Muslim scholars contend this may have contributed to the inclusion of the holy spirit as a part of divinity by most Christians because this angel conveyed messages from God to the prophets.

What happens after death?

Life after Death

According to Islam, Death is the transition of the soul from one realm to another. Death is neither an annihilation nor an extinction. The theme of death is frequent as a reality in the Quran, in the sayings of the Prophet Muhammad, and in other books of the religion. Belief in the life after death is one of the main beliefs of Islam. The soul does not die but the body dies. Death offers an introduction into the unseen world.

In Islam, death symbolizes accountability. Everyone's life is based on accountability. A person has a free will but is accountable for his/her choices. Although there are similarities between Islam and other Judeo-Christian traditions in the belief of afterlife, the day of Judgment, Heaven and punishment, there are also some important differences.

The teachings of the Quran are very much based on the rational persuasion of the reader on the need of the recreation by God and accountability after death. In other words, the Quran expects not only the reader should believe but also should have the certainty of the faith in the afterlife and meeting with God.[24]

Understanding God's attributes also fosters a comprehension of the afterlife. In Islam, God is just and merciful. A person will face accountability in afterlife due to the attribute of God, the Just. At the same time, God is merciful. If a person expects forgiveness, God (the Merciful) can still forgive this person. Therefore, in Islamic creed, there is the uncertainty of not knowing one's fate in afterlife. Uncertainty forms a positive constant struggle to increase in piety and observe the ethical norms until one dies. This internal struggle can be called jihad. The attitude of uncertainty can lead the person to have a piety and virtue, not being arrogant but humble. The sinner can be hopeful because ultimately, the mercy of God saves the person. On the other hand, the just attribute of God encourages a person to strive for high levels of piety and attain great ethical behavior in order to deserve a good compensation from his/her lifelong struggle. Also, the just attribute of God can dissuade and prevent an evil-doer or planner from indulging in illicit acts since there is accountability for such actions.[25]

Islamic theology contends that an individual cannot attain Heaven solely by his/her earthly deeds, but rather only with the mercy of God [10]. Of course, the reward and punishment system presents a motivation to engage in good deeds and avoid evil. However, there shouldn't be any ultimate assertion, perhaps due to implicit or explicit arrogance, that the individual is assured of Heaven solely by his/her efforts.

In Islamic philosophy, a correct understanding of God shows the necessity for life after death. A merciful God does not create a sophisticated system like the universe and complicated beings like humans, and then limit the average lifespan of the latter to seventy years. The innate desire for humans to be eternal is itself a plausible proof that there should be another realm such as the afterlife. In Islamic intellectual reasoning, the practical necessities of an afterlife abounds. To console a child on the loss of a beloved parent, an assurance that he/she will be eventually united with the deceased can ease his/her pains. Likewise, the loneliness of an aged individual who has witnessed the demise of several of his/her peers, can be assuaged by the expectation of a life after death. Surely, a family life will not be on true grounds unless the long shared companionship is not terminated by death but endures with the hope of spending an after-life in heaven.[25]

What is the understanding of evil, good, and destiny?

Destiny, Evil, and Good

According to the Islamic Creed, God knows everything (both past and future) in each individual's life. However, the person has a free will to choose good or evil. God's knowledge of future events does not infer that God forces people to engage in their actions. Everyone is ultimately responsible for his/her actions. Through worship, repentance, and humility, a believer can regularly beseech God to assist him/her in always making the right choices, to do good, and to be protected from evil. For sure, God can answer the person's prayers and God is the "All-Hearing."

This response should be devoid of complaints and the believer should still show continuous appreciation and gratitude to God. Indeed, with greater trials come greater rewards. Islam teaches that those loved by God are often the most tested. During these trials, when the person maintains his/her duties to God with appreciation, gratitude, worship, and prayer, then he/she will be pleased and satisfied. On the contrary, whoever expresses displeasure with the situation, then he/she will be overwhelmed with indignation.[26]

What are the worship requirements in Islam?

Five Worship Pillars of Islam

There are five required pillars of Islam. These are verbal declaration of the oneness of the Creator,[18] daily prayers,[19] fasting,[20] charity,[21] and pilgrimage.[22] All these pillars require the condition of a person being not insane, mentally sound, and being in the age of required maturity, approximately the age of puberty, fifteen years old.

Who is considered a Muslim?

Declaration of Faith

The verbal declaration of oneness of the Creator is the creed of Islam. A Muslim is expected to admit that there is one Creator. This proclamation is "There is no deity but God." In Arabic, this statement is "La ilaha illa Allah." Once a person proclaims the statement and believes it in

---

18. Shahadah.
19. Salah in Arabic and namaz in Indian, Persian, and Turkish cultures.
20. Sawm in Arabic.
21. Zakah in Ar.
22. Hajj in Ar.

his heart, then he/she is considered a Muslim. Recognition of Prophet Muhammad as a messenger of God is also required. The full expression of the declaration of faith is: "There is no deity except God and Muhammad is a messenger and prophet of God." Recognizing Prophet Muhammed as God's emissary suggests all the other messengers and prophets of God are also to be accorded this recognition. With this observation, the full version of the declaration of faith could be: "I believe that there is no deity except only one Creator. I believe in the true message of Muhammad along with other prophets and messengers (Jesus, Moses, Abraham, and others). I believe in all the original and authentic messages of the Quran, the Bible: the Gospel, the Psalms, and the Torah, and all the books truly sent by God. I believe in all the unseen and future events as told by God (the Angels, life after death, etc.), and destiny."

Anyone who has reservations in embodying this core concept of Islam is not considered a true Muslim. There is no requirement of a public announcement of the declaration. However, some of the contemporary scholars encourage new Muslims to declare it openly and publicly in order to benefit from existing community social support groups. Although not required, new Muslims in the West are also often encouraged to change their names for easy integration with the immigrant Muslim communities who mostly bear Arabic names, but lately, this practice is being criticized by some emerging progressive Muslims because the name-change was not a norm during the Prophet's lifetime. The only exception was if the names had unpleasant meanings or connotations.[10]

What are the daily prayers in Islam?

Five Times Daily Prayer

Muslims are required to pray five times daily. Each prayer is a different unit.[23] A unit includes three physical positions with readings of Quranic verses and supplications:

1. Standing Position
2. Bowing Position
3. Prostration

Different positions in daily prayers

---

23. Unit is rakah in Arabic.

A Muslim man praying in the mosque with casual dress

For each prayer, there is a time interval that a Muslim is expected to pray. These are:

1. Morning Prayer:[24] It starts approximately an hour and a half before sunrise, with the real dawn and ends with sunrise.
2. Noon Prayer:[25] It starts approximately an hour after noon when the sun starts declining from the zenith position and lasts approximately three hours. The prayer interval continues until the start of the next prayer (the Afternoon prayer).
3. Afternoon Prayer:[26] It starts at the end of noon prayer and ends with sunset. The prayer interval continues until the start of the next prayer (the Sunset prayer).
4. Sunset Prayer:[27] It starts with sunset and ends after approximately an hour and a half. It continues until the start of the next prayer (the Night prayer).
5. Night Prayer:[28] It starts at the end of the sunset prayer, where the sky totally loses its reddish color due to sunset. It continues until the start of the next prayer (the Morning prayer).

---

24. Fajr prayer.
25. Zuhr Pr.
26. Asr Pr.
27. Magrib Pr.
28. Isha Pr.

Prayer	Start	End
Morning	5:23 am	6:41 am
Noon	1:00 pm	4:35 pm
Afternoon	4:35 pm	7:20 pm
Sunset	7:20 pm	8:38 pm
Night	8:38 pm	5:23 am

Above is an example of prayer times as a daily planner in Manhattan, New York, on April 1, 2018. Muslims find these set times of spiritual "charge" and "discharge" very valuable although it can take a few minutes. [24] The times of the daily prayer change depending on the location and time of the year. The five daily prayers are very crucial in a Muslim's life. Some of the scholars interpret from the saying of the Prophet that a person can have a sound, beneficial, and peaceful belief in God as long as she or he is careful not to miss five daily prayers.

It is required to pray at the time intervals for each prayer. If a person misses a prayer, then it is required for that person to make it up. Each prayer can take up to three to five minutes on average when the minimum conditions of a prayer are fulfilled. If the person cannot prostrate due to physical limitations or illness, he or she may pray in a sitting position or assume any other comfortable posture.

What is Ramadan?

Fasting

Muslims are required to fast once a year for a full month. This month in Arabic is called Ramadan. Muslims follow the lunar calendar; therefore, Ramadan changes each year. During fasting, Muslims are not allowed to eat, drink, or have any sexual relationship from sunrise to sunset. After sunset, all the prohibitions are lifted till sunrise. Due to sickness, old age, or travel engagements, a person may be excused from fasting. In this case, this person is suggested to feed a person daily for each day he or she is unable to fast. The nights of Ramadan are spiritually powerful. Therefore, it was the practice of the Prophet Muhammad to pray after breaking the fast[29] and engage in long prayers. To sustain this practice,

---

29. This prayer is called tarawih in Arabic.

Muslims get together during Ramadan, pray on each night of this month and recite the Quran in abundance.

Are Muslims required to give charity?

Charity

Muslims are required to give 2.5% of their excess wealth to other people in need. The excess money is the amount after one fulfills his or her basic needs of food, housing, and transportation. After these needs, 2.5% of any excess should be given to the poor every year. Anyone without any such excess is not obligated to engage in this act of charity. In lieu of cash, there are also stipulated levies for those in possession of livestocks, jeweleries, etc.

What is the Muslim's pilgrimage or Hajj?

Pilgrimage

A Muslim is required to visit the holy sites once in his or her lifetime. This requirement exists if the person has the financial means to travel and can support his or her family during his or her absence. If the person does not have enough financial means, then this person is not required to perform a pilgrimage. Another condition for this religious obligation is that the intending pilgrim should be in good health for travel.

The Kabah

The Kaabah is a small building cubicle located in the city of Makkah, Saudi Arabia. Islamic traditions assert that the building was initially built by Prophet Adam, and that Prophet Abraham and his son, Prophet Ishmael, rebuilt it. During prayers, Muslims face towards the direction of the Kaabah. Hence, mosques (Muslim places of worship) are built in a direction aligning with the Kaabah.

Muslims visit the Kabah during the pilgrimage. As part of worship, they circumambulate the Kaabah, make supplications, and sit around it. Muslims view the Kabah as a symbol of respect.[30] In the beginning

---

30. Shai'r in Ar.

of Islam, early Muslims used to pray toward Jerusalem as part of the Abrahamic religion. Later, with an order from God in the Quran, the direction was changed to the Kaabah.

Praying towards the Kaabah five times a day affords Muslims to develop a sense of geographical awareness. Irrespective of their current location (their homes, place of work, or even during travel), Muslims are compelled to be aware of current cardinal directions (North, South, East, or West) in order to properly identify the direction of the Kaabah.

In Islam, The Kaabah is a symbolic representation that establishes the concept of a sacred structure that Prophet Abraham had built (or repaired) solely for the worship of God. Some non-Muslims may inadvertently think that Muslims worship the building. On the contrary, the building as envisioned by Abraham is a place to gather and commemorate the worship of God alone (Monotheism). Muslims don't worship the Kaabah but use it for directional purposes to establish unity and structure in their prayers. The choice of the Kaabah for such purpose was ordered by God. According to one of the narrations from the Prophet Muhammad, the Kaabah is the first temple of worship on earth dedicated to the worship of One (and only) God.[10] In Islamic legal and theological system, the worth of a human exceeds that of the Kaabah. This clearly indicates that for Muslims, the Kaabah is just a sacred object.

MECCA, SAUDI ARABIA—Muslim pilgrims from all around the world circumambulating the Kabah on January 29, 2017.

What are the similarities and differences between Islam, Judaism, and Christianity?

Comparing Islam with Christianity, Judaism, and other Religions

In Islam, God is one. God has different names and attributes. God is the Merciful. God is the Loving and Loved one. God is the Preserver, the Real King, and the Knower. There are many attributes of God. Although "He" is used to refer to God, God is neither He nor She.

Christianity, Judaism, and Islam are classified as Abrahamic religions. These three religions acknowledge Abraham as their common ancestor or prophet and accept his teachings. Abraham is an embodiment of the belief in One God. Therefore, Christianity, Judaism, and Islam are all monotheistic religions. Along with their substantial commonalities, they also have some differences. Some of them are summarized in the table following.

	Judaism	Christianity	Islam
Belief in One God	✓	✓	✓
Trinity		✓	
Belief in Prophets/Messengers	✓	✓	✓
Belief in Afterlife	✓	✓	✓
Belief in Accountability	✓	✓	✓
Belief in Angels	✓	✓	✓
Divinity of Jesus		✓	
Prophethood or Messengership of Jesus		✓	✓
Jesus as the Messiah		✓	✓
Miracle Birth of Jesus		✓	✓
Second Coming of Jesus		✓	✓

	Judaism	Christianity	Islam
Concept of Original Sin		✓	
Moses as the Messenger of God	✓	✓	✓
Abraham as the Messenger of God	✓	✓	✓

Source: Dr. Y. J. Kumek

The check marks denote the commonalities among these three religions; however, their understanding and interpretation of any shared or common belief are often different.

Also, similar accounts of some historical events or incidents are mentioned in the Quran, the Old and New Testaments. Some of these include the narratives about God's messengers/prophets (Moses, David, Abraham, Jonah, Solomon, Noah, etc.), the creation of Adam and his interaction with Satan, the creation of the universe in six days, and many others.

Muslims accept Jesus as a prophet sent by God. Islam teaches that Jesus came with a message and book from God to revive and reinstate the original message from God. Unlike Christianity, Islam does not believe in the notion of an "original" sin. In Islam, Adam is regarded as a noble prophet of God. Adam and Eve were sent to earth, not as a punishment to atone for a past misdeed, but on a test mission of their faith (along with their progeny). Therefore, their coming down to earth was an ascension and not a spiritual descent due to a sin.

Are the Muslims in America and Europe different?

Islam in the West

Islam has become a major religion in America and Europe. Different groups constitute the identity of Muslims in America and Europe: Immigrant Muslims, Second (and later) generation Muslims, and converted Muslims. The Immigrant Muslims are those who migrated from their home countries. Second (and later) generation Muslims are descendants of the immigrant Muslims who were born in America or Europe. They try to combine their Western culture with the native cultures of their parents. The convert Muslims are those who adopt Islam as a new way of life. Some famous Muslims are Muhammad Ali and Mike Tyson (boxers), Cat Stevens (singer, with his new name Yusuf Islam), Dr. Oz (Medical Doctor), and Kareem Abdul-Jabbar (NBA basketball player).

The immigrant Muslims who migrated to the West have continuously established their own institutions (schools, places of worships, etc.), and have been integrated into the social life in the West. Their descendants are playing increasingly greater roles in their society's economic, political, and educational systems, forming the identities of "American Muslims" and "European Muslims." This identity is more dominant in America where there is no single prevailing nationality in the country.

The Muslim institutions are either predominantly ethnic based or a mixture of ethnicities. In the places where a Muslim ethnicity is dominant, it is expected to see a mosque to reflect the culture of that ethnicity in the understanding of the religion. For example, in a mosque with a majority Arab or Indian culture, it is common to see women wearing black, colorful, or traditional clothes. On the other hand, the mosques with attendees of Bosnian or Turkish culture would mostly have casual dress while attending the mosque. In some of the metropolitan cities, it is easy to see the very mixture of different cultures and ethnicities in the worship places and services. On page 38 is a traditionally Bosnian structured mosque in Uttica, New York. The green preference is possibly present in the structure to reflect the favorite color of Prophet Muhammad.

Annual celebration prayers (ei'd) can be in any spacious indoor or outdoor place. An example of this prayer is in a basketball stadium in Windsor, Canada, as presented below. The mixture of different ethnicities is very vivid in the picture below. In general, Muslims often rent huge spaces such as stadiums to hold thousands of people in their locality during their annual celebration prayers.

A Bosnian mosque in Utica, New York, United States

What is the place of societal customs and culture in Islam?

Customs and Culture

Both women and men tend to reflect their personal proclivities and individual cultural preferences in their understanding (and interpretation) of Islamic teachings. This reflection can be in worship places, social life, and professional environments. Islamic teachings are not there to change the culture or tradition[31] as long as such practices do not conflict with basic premises such as belief in One Creator, justice, free choice, and individual rights.

Are Muslims violent?

Violence

Islam, an Abrahamic religion whose name literally means "peace and submission," and Muslims, who adopt these teachings, continuously and regularly face challenges from violent elements using their names to commit heinous acts. According to Muslim sources,[27] a small but loud group is committing inhuman actions of violence in the name of their faith. According to them, modern media have been overlooking the voices of the millions of Muslims who are horrified by these events.

---

31. Urf.

The Quran and the practices of the Prophet of Islam, Muhammad, harshly warn against any type of behavior that provokes fear and resentments. The Quran and hadith, scholarly records of the Prophet's actions and reactions, as well as the works of Islamic scholars, very clearly condemn all sorts of violent acts. According to Muslims, Muhammad is a role model for all mankind, and sincere efforts to emulate his character are an important aspect of Islam. He strongly opposed malicious violence and his views were based upon the Quranic verse that equates the killing of an innocent person with killing all humanity [Quran 5:32].

According to Karen Armstrong,[8] the Prophet Muhammad clearly demonstrated respect for ethnic and religious diversity. To give an example, he stood to honor the funeral parade of a Jewish man, and by doing so, taught people to respect humans for their moral attributes, regardless of their faith. He also allowed Christians of Najran to perform their prayers right in his mosque in Madina which exemplifies religious tolerance. Muhammad's guests were from all ethnic and religious (Christians, Jews, Zoroastrians, and polytheists) backgrounds. All were respected and treated honorably in his presence. He offered non-binding advice to all communities. Despite the current wave of destruction in the name of religion, the relics of ancient religions and communities of non-Muslims were safe in Muslim lands for hundreds of years under Islamic rule. This testifies to the respect Muslims have had for the pre-Muslim past and to the sublime and accommodating nature of the religion.[28]

So how is it possible that a religion that so strongly promotes peace and dialogue can be manipulated to such a degree that vulnerable young Muslims are drawn into violence? There have been many historical incidents where self-proclaimed religious leaders manipulated the emotions of the ignorant masses for a political objective. These orators speak charismatically in the name of God, to provoke feelings of fear and guilt, leading to catastrophic events. This was true for Islam, Christianity, and Judaism. Using passages out of context from holy books and exploiting them to incite violent behavior is not a new occurrence, and the Quran is not the first of the sacred texts to be abused in this way.

"Read" is the first verse revealed to Prophet Muhammad [96:1]. Education offers us the possibility of resolving many human problems including the mistaken views of violence in Islam. Muslims believe that there are currently far too few opportunities to expand one's knowledge about Islam beyond the news industry, which often sensationalizes violent actions of some Muslims, committed in the name of Islam. According to some emerging scholars in the West,[17] this education should focus upon the original teachings of the Quran and genuine practices of Muhammad with their accurate interpretations. There is an overwhelming consensus in Islamic scholarly traditions against violence. Therefore, Muslim youth should be equipped with these foundations to help distinguish between the original teachings of Islam and feigned ideas, and thus, prevent any type of deceptive manipulation.

Islam consists of a diversity of sects and perspectives and all, save a few, condemn violence. Muslims are increasing their efforts in the West to take leadership in educating their communities with the peaceful teachings of Islam. There is an increasing and positive awareness towards religious education of the possibly vulnerable groups in the West by Muslim civil groups. The government agencies regularly support these initiatives of education. These agencies have positively increased their efforts to connect with Muslim grassroots organizations to increase the awareness of the horrible effects of violence.

What is Islamic Law?

Law, Society, and Politics

There are detailed guidelines of worship, social, and family relationships for an ethical and peaceful life in Islam. The fundamental methodology to establish these guidelines is by studying the Quran, by the sayings and practices of the Prophet Muhammad,[32] by the consensus of the scholars on a matter, and by using logic and critical thinking. It is important to understand the systemization and canonization of these methods and later formation of different legal schools or madhabs[33] in Islamic history. These guidelines are markedly based on basic universal values such as not to transgress the rights of other humans, animals, trees, or the environment. The goal of these guidelines and rulings is to establish

---
32. Referred to as hadith and Sunnah.
33. Such as Hanafi, Shafii, Maliki, Hanbali schools.

balance as practiced by the Prophet. Historically, depending on the time and location, volumes of books have been written to systematize the teachings of the Quran and the sayings and practices of the Prophet Muhammad. This continually updated systemization, such as the constitution of a country, helped the following generations understand the occurrences with their relation to the context, time, person, and their specificity and generalizability of the occurrences. This systemization is called Islamic law.[34] One of the motivating reasons to establish guidelines after the demise of the Prophet and earlier generations was to prevent literal and wrong interpretations of the Quran and sayings and practices of the Prophet Muhammad. As mentioned for religious texts and scriptures, following the letter (scripture) but not spirit of the letter could be deadly.[17] This saying indicates the importance of not following religious scriptures literally but with scholarly, contextual, and sound interpretations.

What is Sufism?

Sufism

Sufism is the deeper understanding and practice of one's relation with God. According to some Sufis, people are spirits in physical bodies.[22] A person who establishes an intimate relationship with God sets a goal of a spiritual journey to please God. This lifelong struggle or journey until death is generally characterized or named as Sufism by the Westerners and called "Tasawwuf" by some Muslims. Sufism describes the structural outline of this spiritual journey; although some of the Muslim sholars may not be in favor of this type of characterization. People have a need to fulfill the spiritual hunger. If the person doesn't care about spiritual sustenance from a pure source then the soul will take it from a poisonous source.

A Sufi teacher can be viewed as a personal spiritual trainer. The Sufi teacher's[35] goal is to teach and diagnose a person's sickness of the heart, soul, and other spiritual faculties. With practice and knowledge, the

---
34. Referred to as Fiqh by the Muslims or mostly Shariah by the Westerners.
35. Murshid in terminology.

person becomes a better human being in the sight of God and for other humans, and for living and non-living things. For example, one of the Sufi Masters say that

> "I don't throw a scratch paper in the garbage with other garbage materials. I fold it nicely put it in a separate place due to my respect to knowledge, to the tree that the paper was made of and to the Creator who gave all those for my service."

The actions and thought processes of Sufis are not often considered the norm but are usually viewed as extraordinary by others. The concept of ethical and spiritual perfection is summarized with one of the famous Sufi sayings, "Good deeds of pious are the disobedience of the elect ones."[29] This means that every person's spiritual journey is individualized and there is no end to climb up in the spiritual journey. An example of this can be of two students. One student comes late to the class and it is good that he still came to the class even though it was late for the teacher. On the other hand, for a punctual and good student, coming late to the class can be an act of disobedience to the teacher.

Whirling Dervish Performance

Prayer beads are used to engage in chanting

Some Sufis interpret the death as the wedding day of the loved and the beloved,[24] meaning the mystical union of the person and God. Some of the essentials in Sufism are good teachers and good company. These are the two main vehicles to remind the main teaching of Sufism in the journey to the Loved, God. The discourses of the Loved, God, is all the type of genuine conversations, experiences, reflections, and feelings that would help the spiritual traveler to get closer and closer to God until the person dies. Any type of unrelated indulgence, conversations, experience, thoughts, reflections, and feelings are considered null and insignificant if it is not serving this purpose of intimate relationship with the Loved, God.

What is the role of women in Islam?

Women

It is important to analyze the status of women in the society before and after Islam. Before Islam, in the desert Arabian region women were much oppressed and were exploited mostly as a commodity. Female infanticide was very common, which is also mentioned in the verses of the Quran [81:9]. Women were not able to inherit and did not have any public respect and position with very few exceptions.[8] With the advent of Islam, one of the main critics raised against Muhammad by his contemporaries was his liberal expressions about women. One of the Prophet Muhammad's early critics said, "Look Muhammad, he is changing all our values. He is even giving rights to the women."[8]

After Islam, women have gained important roles in the society and family. The practice of Prophet Muhammad encouraged and supported the self-stance of women in the society. His wife, Aisha, was a very prominent intellectual. She later became the commander chief (top general) of the army after the Prophet's demise in a critical war in the Muslim history.[30] This was totally novel in that society, a woman leading an army. Amongst many others, another example of Islam's respect for women is the establishment of a prominent institution of higher learning in honor of a woman. Several years after Prophet Muhammad's demise, an advanced institution (Al-Azhar) dedicated to the learning and propagation of Islamic sciences was established in Egypt to honor the prophet's daughter, Fatimah. Considered one of the first universities in the world, Al-Azhar is widely renowned as Islam's most prestigious university and it also oversees a national network of schools in Egypt. Currently, thousands of students graduate from this institution each year. This institution has a very high reputation among Muslims and non-Muslims.

Although there are very strong teachings to prevent the abuse of the women and the encouragement for the minority representations, the cultural expectations sometimes intervene with religious teachings and unfortunately one can still see lots of unfortunate issues revolving around women's rights in the Islamic society and family life today. One of the famous sayings of the Prophet Muhammad that circulates in the Muslim sermons is that "The best of you is the one who is in best treatment of his family (wife)."[10] There is an increasing movement of especially educated women both in the West and other parts of the world challenging androcentric and patriarchal interpretation of the religious teachings. The emergence of women religious scholars is promising as a positive effort of removing cultural and masculine subjective interpretations from the primary teachings in the Quran and the hadith.[31]

In a family life, Islamic legal law stipulates that the financial responsibilities are required to be borne by the man. The wife has the right to work but she is not obliged to bear any of the household expenses (including her own expenses). If she decides to contribute, then it is considered charity on her part. In other words, according to Islamic teachings, the responsibility of home financial maintenance solely rests on the man's shoulders.

In gender interpretation of women, it is recognized that women are natural givers and make a lot of sacrifice, especially in childbearing and upbringing. Islam recognizes that the gender-related needs of women can be different from their male counterparts. Hence, in comparison to men, the sacred legal responsibilities of women are less. For example, a woman is not obliged to attend the weekly Friday prayers. While this religious responsibility is required for men, it is only optional or discretionary for women. Also, a woman on her menstruation cycle does not need to pray or fast.

In Muslim discourses of the gender, a woman in Islam is generally depicted with her spiritual and physical beauty. Therefore, the textual and oral discourses emerge to prevent the abuse of the woman physically and spiritually. One can find these explicit teachings in the verses of the Quran and in the sayings of the Prophet Muhammad. Therefore, Muslim women practice the Islamic teachings of the dress code in order to implement modesty in their personal life and not to be exploited physically due to their gender. One of the examples that Muslim women take as their role model is the mother of Jesus, Virgin Mary. They believe she observed a similar modest dress code. Therefore, they emulate Virgin Mary in every aspect.[32]

In response to emerging modern needs, especially regarding the migration of Muslims to non-Muslim lands, contemporary Muslim scholarship advocates the Islamic principle that Muslims should follow the law and tenets of the country they currently reside. However, if the law(s) require them to engage in unlawful acts, the Quran advises that Muslims should migrate to another land and seek an alternate residence. With this perspective, most Muslim women in the West rationalize that the permissibility granted to men in marrying multiple spouses (maximum of four) in the Quran is simply discretionary and should be only applicable under special circumstances. Hence, Muslim men should not break the law by having more than one wife if the existing law in their country of residence does not permit polygamy. According to normative exegesis of the Quran, the sacred text not only corroborates this interpretation on the discretionary nature of polygamy, but actually advises monogamy. Amongst a few others, an example for the exceptional permissibility of polygamy is a situation whereby women needed protection through marriage, especially in tribal or feudal societies.

A Muslim woman praying in a mosque

How are the contemporary social ethics issues viewed?

Social Ethics

One can look at today's social ethics issues in Islam as well as such things as drugs, alcohol, abortion, LGBTQ rights, dating, marriage, extramarital affairs, and many others.

As a general rule of methodology,[36] Islamic ethical and legal guidelines implicitly and explicitly intends to benefit the individual, the society, and the living and non-living things at-large on the earth and in the universe. These very basic principles are historically established methodologies with the teachings of the Quran, sayings and practices of the Prophet Muhammad and later, with the institutionalized schools of law and practice.[37] Some of the underlining basic principles are protecting individual rights, freedom, honor, and property. Then, the benefit of the society[38] at-large can occur, but without transgressing these basic

---

36. Usul.
37. Called Mazhabs.
38. Urf or Maslaha.

individual rights. There have always been the positive and constructive friction of this hardly balanced pendulum, swinging between the individual and social benefits when decisions and enforcements prevail. In other words, in Islamic social ethics, one cannot harm or kill one person to benefit one hundred people. One cannot pursue a virtuous goal with evil means. In other words, all the steps to achieve a virtuous end should also be virtuous.

In the personal affairs, the type of benefit or transgression is classified into two categories: the issues related to the individual and God, and the issues related to the individual and other humans and beings. One can call this vertical, transcendent relation with God and horizontal relationship with humans. Everyone has the free will to choose what he/she wants to believe and what he/she wants to do. The Quran repeats and highlights the concept of transgression or wrong.[39] Transgression or relationship emerges in two types: vertical (related to the Creator) and horizontal (related to the people). Transgression against the Creator does not bear any accountability in this world. This transgression is mainly not recognizing God as the Creator and consequently not appreciating God's favors. The second type of transgression is against human dignity on social justice. It could involve invidious discrimination by race, ethnicity, or religion. The Quran suggests law enforcement measures to remove this type of transgression. Some Islamic social scholars, such as Fazlur Rahman,[33] suggest that legal rulings for law enforcement could be secular as long as the laws are fair, just, and transparent which is the essential objective of the Quranic legal system.[40] As the result of both types of offenses, according to Quranic teachings, the person in reality wrongs, oppresses, or transgresses, himself or herself.[41] There is no compulsion in the choice of belief or religion as mentioned in the verses of the Quran [2:256]. Islam has in some ways similar and in some ways different understanding of the social ethic issues with other Abrahamic religions: normative Christianity and normative Judaism.

In these rulings, for example, drugs can be used for medical purposes. Although limited consumption of alcohol can have benefits, due to the weakness of the individual's self-control and its possible adversary

---

39. Zulm.
40. Sharia.
41. Nafs- wa lakinna anfusahum yazlimun in Arabic repeated in different parts of the Quran.

effects to the society, the rulings discourage and try to stop usage of alcohol. The formation of a baby in the mother's womb and its timelines are implicitly and explicitly expressed in the Quran. Therefore, the cases of abortion are considered individually case by case depending on the medical need, the stage of the trimester of the baby, and the reasons of abortion if it is a choice without any reason. In Islamic legal normative books written centuries ago,[42] there are extensive sections about similar cases of LGBTQ issues. The arguments can take each case separately especially with the medical cases of "khunnas" similar somehow to what is defined as LGBTQ today. On the other hand, without any proven medical impulse, if there is a choice by the individual to be LGBT then it is considered as sin between the person and God. Islam recognizes the case of LGBT as the sin between the person and the Creator, as well as it may have some social effects to the protection of collective rights such as spread of diseases. In the cases of extramarital affairs, the guidelines are present to establish fair, reputable, and healthy societies based on healthy families. Marital and kinship relationships are to protect the rights of children and women but at the same time encouraging men to establish long-term happy and mutual beneficial relationships for all the stakeholders.

In all of the above cases and in other social ethics issues, the normative Islamic understanding is that there is no hate to the sinner but there is a disapproval and dislike to the action.

What is the place of Art, Education, and Science in Islam?

Art, Education, and Science

One can observe the reflections of Islamic art in different parts of the social, educational, and professional life. Calligraphy and linguistic art are examples Islamic influences on the society. One can observe the stylistic writings of the verses and name of God in the walls of mosques and in picture frames in the houses, vehicles, stores, and offices of the Muslims. One can observe different Islamic monuments, temples, and prayer carpets reflecting the culture with Islamic motifs.

---

42. By Imam Abu Hanifah, Shafili Malik, and in their commentaries such as in Hidayah.[71]

Linguistic art can be observed in the traditional composition of poems and writings, especially inspired by the words, styles, and teachings of the Quran and sayings of the prophets. One should have the knowledge of semantics, knowledge of figures of speech like similes and metaphors, and knowledge of the rhetoric to understand the phase constructions, implicit and explicit meanings which reveal the beauty of the language and its implications. In Muslim countries, there is a substantial habit of listening to the Quranic recitation similar to listening to music.

In Islam, education is very crucial. There are a lot of prophetic sayings that emphasize the importance of education. In one of the famous sayings of the Prophet Muhammad: "For Satan, it is 1,000 times more difficult to give temptations and false guidance to an educated scholar than to an uneducated naive worshipper.[26]" Islam encourages Muslims to be educated in their religion and sciences, and not to be blind followers. In this saying of the Prophet, a God-conscious scholar has a higher level than a pious worshipper who is less educated. In one other saying of the Prophet Muhammad, it is mentioned that irrespective of sex, learning is incumbent on all Muslims.[34]

The Quran especially emphasizes reflection and critical analysis on scientific events and nature in order to acknowledge God. The Quran states that the scholars who have knowledge and education are the real believers that have the fear, respect, awe, and love of God. Historically, Muslims did not have a problem with science rather they were encouraged to look for different cosmological, microscopic, and macroscopic events with scientific knowledge due to the encouragement of many verses in the Quran. One can find many verses of the Quran about different disciplines of natural, humanities, and social sciences such as embryology, biology, astronomy, zoology, chemistry, sociology, logic, philosophy, and literature.[35]

A window in Morocco in a historical mosque.

What is Halal?

The Muslim's Diet: Permissible and Impermissible

Halal is permissible and haram is impermissible in food and other religious legal categorizations. Therefore, one can find "halal" labels in Muslims' food items. Similar to Jewish tradition, Muslims don't eat pork and wild animals. There is an understanding that the effect of the food can have an effect not only on the physical body but also on metaphysical faculties of a person.[24] A person engaged in permissible, halal, will find ease in his/her prayers and in following the commands of God. On the contrary, the person who is eating and dealing with the impermissible may not feel the same desire to establish relationship with God and perform prayers. This person can become unethical in his/her relationships with people and God. In Islam, the number of impermissible items are much fewer than the permissible ones. Although one can find a lot of books on the wisdom and the possible reasons of impermissible items, Muslims are required to distinguish between halal (permissible) with haram (impermissible) with submissive attitude to God.

In social life, there are impermissible and permissible items as well according to Islamic value system. It is permissible and commendable to loan money to someone but it is impermissible to get interest from it. It is impermissible to gamble and drink alcohol. It is impermissible and a huge sin to kill an innocent person, lie, cheat, backbite, and slander. It is not permissible being full while the neighbor is hungry.

If a Muslim performs any of the impermissible actions, then this person is classified as a sinner. The accountability for this action is between this person and God. This person can ask repentance from God any time before death. If the transgression or evil is related to others' rights, then this person should seek the means of forgiveness in this world from these individuals in addition to asking forgiveness from God.

Halal fast-food stand sale in Manhattan, New York

PART 2
SELECTED PASSAGES
FROM THE QURAN
WITH INTERPRETED MEANINGS

The Names of Chapters in the Quran

1	Al-Fatiha	The Opening
2	Al-Baqarah	The Cow Story
3	Al-'Imran	The Family of Imran
4	An-Nisa'	The Women
5	Al-Ma'idah	The Feast
6	Al-An'am	The Cattle
7	Al-A'raf	The Elevated Places
8	Al-Anfal	Voluntary Gifts
9	At-Taubah	The Repentance
10	Yunus	Jonah
11	Hud	Hud
12	Yusuf	Joseph
13	Ar-Ra'd	The Thunder
14	Ibrahim	Abraham
15	Al-Hijr	The Place of Rocks
16	An-Nahl	The Bee
17	Al-Isra	The Night Journey
18	Al-Kahf	The Cave
19	Maryam	Jesus's Mother Virgin Mary
20	Ta Ha	The Letters T, H
21	Al-Anbiya'	The Prophets
22	Al-Hajj	The Pilgrimage
23	Al-Mu'minun	The Believers
24	An-Nur	The Light
25	Al-Furqan	The Separator
26	Ash-Shu'ara'	The Poets
27	An-Naml	The Ant
28	Al-Qasas	The Narrative
29	Al-'Ankabut	The Spider
30	Ar-Rum	The Romans

31	Luqman	Luqman, The Wise
32	As-Sajdah	The Prostration
33	Al-Ahzab	The Allies
34	Al-Saba'	The Sheba
35	Al-Fatir	The Originator
36	Ya Sin	The Letters Y, S
37	As-Saffat	Those Ranging in Ranks
38	Sad	The Letter S
39	Az-Zumar	The Companies
40	Al-Mu'min	The Believer
41	HaMim	The Letters H, M
42	Ash-Shura	The Counsel
43	Az-Zukhruf	The Gold
44	Ad-Dukhan	The Smoke
45	Al-Jathiyah	The Kneeling
46	Al-Ahqaf	The Sandhills
47	Muhammad	Muhammad
48	Al-Fath	The Victory
49	Al-Hujurat	The Apartments
50	Qaf	The letter Q
51	Ad-Dhariyat	The Scatterers
52	At-Tur	The Mountain
53	An-Najm	The Star
54	Al-Qamar	The Moon
55	Ar-Rahman	The All Merciful
56	Al-Waqi'ah	The Event
57	Al-Hadid	The Iron
58	Al-Mujadilah	The Woman in Appeal
59	Al-Hashr	The Gathering
60	Al-Mumtahanah	The Examined
61	As-Saff	The Ranks
62	Al-Jumu'ah	The Friday Congregation

63	Al-Munafiqun	The Hypocrites
64	At-Taghabun	Mutual Loss
65	At-Talaq	Divorce
66	At-Tahrim	The Prohibition
67	Al-Mulk	The Authority
68	Al-Qalam	The Pen
69	Al-Haqqah	The Reality
70	Al-Ma'arij	The Ways of Ascent
71	Nuh	Noah
72	Al-Jinn	The Unseen Beings
73	Al-Muzzammil	The Covered One
74	Al-Muddaththir	The Cloaked One
75	Al-Qiyamah	The Resurrection
76	Al-Insan	The Man
77	Al-Mursalat	Those Sent Forth
78	An-Naba'	The News
79	An-Nazi'at	The Pullers
80	'Abasa	The One Who Frowned
81	At-Takwir	The Folding Up
82	Al-Infitar	The Cleaving
83	mutafifeen	The Fraud
84	Al-Inshiqaq	The Massive Explosion
85	Al-Buruj	The Sea of Stars
86	At-Tariq	The Morning Star
87	Al-A'laa	The Most High
88	Al-Ghashiyah	The Overwhelming Event
89	Al-Fajr	The Daybreak
90	Al-Balad	The City
91	Ash-Shams	The Sun
92	Al-Lail	The Night
93	Ad-Duha	The Morning Hour

PART 2   Selected Passages from the Quran with Interpreted Meanings

94	Al-Inshirah	The Chest Expansion
95	At-Tin	The Fig
96	Al-'Alaq	The Embryo
97	Al-Qadr	The Power
98	Al-Bayyinah	The Clear Proof
99	Al-Zilzal	The Earthquake
100	Al-'Adiyat	The Raiders
101	Al-Qari'ah	The Calamity
102	At-Takathur	The Greed
103	Al-'Asr	The Time
104	Al-Humazah	The Slanderer
105	Al-Fil	The Elephant
106	Al-Quraish	The Tribe of Quraish
107	Al-Ma'un	The Small Kindness
108	Al-Kauthar	The Abundance
109	Al-Kafirun	The Ungrateful Ones
110	An-Nasr	The Help
111	Al-Lahab	The Flame
112	Al-Ikhlas	The Unity
113	Al-Falaq	The Dawn
114	An-Nas	The Mankind

The above table presents the chapter numbers and names of the Quran with their original Arabic names and their translated possible meanings, chosen from among different possibilities. In this book, at least one verse from each chapter of the Quran is selected to introduce the unfamiliar English reader to the main sacred text of Islam. Rather than using the above original chapter names, this book uses selected theme(s) of the verses as titles for each chapter, accompanied with the original chapter numbers. While the first number in the brackets denotes the above chapter numbers, the second number denotes the verse numbers within the chapter.

Table of Different Names of the Quran

Below is a table of different names and attributes of the Quran which are mentioned in the Quran itself in different chapters and verses [39] [40]. In other words, the Quran calls itself with different names in its own text. Each name of the Quran occurs in the Quran with different repetitive numbers. The most repeated name is "the Quran" which can be translated as "that (book) which is read a lot." The next recurring name is "the Book." In Islamic theology, the revelation is a book, the universe is a book, and the human being is a book. All the books triangulate together and they are complementary [25]. The next frequent name is "the Descended Revelation from God" which is repeated constantly to tell the reader that this sacred Book is not made up by a human such as Muhammad, but revealed and descended to humans from God. The next repetitive name is "the Reminder" that the Quran is a reminder for the one who is wise and can take advice. The next repeated name is "the Right Guidance" which the Quran is a guidance for the seeker. The next recurrent name is "the truth" that is reiterated in the Quran to remind the reader that all content of the Quran is the truth and there is no doubt. The next frequent name is "the Confirming Scripture of the Bible: the Gospel, the Psalms, and the Torah, and Previous Scriptures Sent by God" which tells the reader that the message in the Quran is not something new but confirms the original messages of the previous scriptures sent by God such as the Bible, Torah, and others. The below table presents different names of the Quran presented in the Quran itself with the number of occurrences in the text.

PART 2   Selected Passages from the Quran with Interpreted Meanings

	Different Names of the Quran in the Quran and their Translation		Number of occurrences in the Quran
1	Al-Kitab	The Book	27
2	Mubin	The Clarifier	5
3	Al-Quran	The Quran	30
4	Karim	Honorable, Noble	1
5	Kalam Allah	The Word of God	1
6	Nur	Sacred Light	3
7	Al-Huda	The Guidance	11
8	Rahmah	Mercy	5
9	Al-Furqan	The Criterion	3
10	As-Shifa	The Healer	3
11	Maw'iza	Admonition	3
12	Dhikr	The Reminder	12
13	Mubarak	Blessed	4
14	Al'i	The Exalted	1
15	Al-Hikmah	The Wisdom	1
16	Al-Hakim	The Full of Wisdom	4
17	Al-Muhaymin	The Guardian of the Bible: the Gospel, the Psalms, and the Torah	1
18	Musaddiq	Conforming Scripture of the Bible: the Gospel, the Psalms, and the Torah	7
19	Hablillah	The Rope of God	1
20	Sirat al mustaqim	The Straight Path	1
21	Qayyim	Straight Guidance	1
22	Qawl	The Word	2
23	Al-Fasl	The Separator	1
24	Nabaun Azam	Supreme Message	2
25	Ahsan ul Hadith	The Best Message	1
26	Mathani	The Repeated	1
27	Mutashabih	Consistent in Itself	1

28	Tanzil	The Descended Revelation	14
29	Ruh	The Book which Gives Life to Faith	1
30	Wahy	The Revelation	4
31	Arabi	In Arabic	6
32	Basair	The Discernment	2
33	Bayan	The Final Statement	1
34	Ilm	Unlimited Knowledge	2
35	Haqq	The Truth, True	10
36	Hadi	The Guide	3
37	Ajab	Wonderful	1
38	Tadhkira	Admonition, Reminder	3
39	Urwatul Wuthqa	The Firm Handhold	1
40	Sidq	The Truth	2
41	Al-Adl	The Justice	1
42	AmrAllah	The Commandment of God	1
43	Munadi	Inviter to the Faith	1
44	Bushra	Glad Tidings	4
45	Majid	The Glorious	2
46	Zabur	The Scripture	1
47	Bashir	Herald of Glad Tidings	2
48	Nadhir	The Warner	1
49	Aziz	The Mighty	1
50	Balagh	The Sufficient Message	2
51	Qasas	Narratives	1
52	Suhuf	The Scripture	2
53	Mukarrama	The Honored	1
54	Marfua	Exalted	1
55	Mutahhara	Kept Pure	2

Notes on Transliteration and Translated Interpretive Meanings

This book uses a contextual translation approach as explained in detail in the appendix about the translation technique. In this method, the translator tries to give an intended meaning of the verse by analyzing the traditional and contemporary exegetical meanings[43] in order to carry it into today's everyday English language. Although it is not easy to give interpretive meanings to Quranic verses, my effort and intention was to decrease the barriers of understandability and clarity for some of the verses of the Quran. It is well known that the difficulty of translation with interpretive meanings is due to many genres of the Quranic Arabic, the content, the style, the context, the audience, the inclusivity and the exclusivity, the legality, the clear and implicit meanings, and others.

The available and popular English translations were analyzed. Here is the methodology that I followed: In most of the verses, in the beginning I tried to translate without looking at other translations. After the translation was completed, I reviewed other renderings in other translations for the selected verses. Most of the time due to the archaic, non-contextual, unclear, and improper choice of words of the available translations, I preferred to use the interpreted exegetical contemporary as this methodology is detailed in the appendix section of this book.

In these interpreted meanings, the selected translations in this book may show an effort to minimize the incorrect renderings about God due to the figurative language in the original language of Arabic when translated into the target language of English. Some scholars can refer this as the method of "tanzih," knowing first who God is not, then, knowing who God is. For example, below is an excerpt from this book for the translation of the word "Rabb" which comes frequently in the Quran:

> Rabb is translated as "God, the Originator, Upholder and Maintainer" for the chapter of Opening (Fatiha). With the exception of Asad's translation, classical translations [5][6][4][3] [2][7] for Rabb in other texts generally prefer the English word,

---

43. Tafsir in Arabic

"Lord"[1] Lord in classical English can refer to the authority and ownership with slavery with negative embedded meanings[8]. Also, in Christian theology, Lord usually refers to Jesus, which may cause confusion to the unfamiliar reader. One of the common words in daily usage of this word is related to the owner of a property referred to as the landlord which can have reductive meanings for the general English reader. Oppositely, in Arabic, Rabb has many meanings such as upbringing, nourishing, teaching, making order, upkeeping, caregiving, controlling, safeguarding, and maintaining with love, mercy, and care. Therefore, the best example of this can be the usage when parents have a relationship with their child with all these qualities of the word rabb with love, mercy, and care. In this text, depending on the context, different attributes of God embedded in the attribute of Rabb are chosen and used. M. Asad's translation [1] uses Sustainer as the translation of Rabb, which is a very good attempt to change the traditional vocabulary for this word. However, depending on the context, I think it is most appropriate to use alternate meanings of the word.

I had the intention and effort of translating all the words into English to eliminate alienation for the unfamiliar and general readers. For example, the name of "Allah" is translated as God to minimize the confusion although it may not give the exact meaning. The Prophet Muhammad is sometimes referred to as the Prophet. I tried to avoid parenthesis in the translations to make the text user-friendly for the unfamiliar readers of the scriptures. To increase the flow, the proper adverbs are placed within the intended and contextual meaning of the original language. I tried to give immediate contextual apparent explicit meanings (zahir) compared to their implicit (batin) ones although it is always arguable by the exegetical scholars what can be explicit and implicit.

As outlined in existing translations of the Quran, I want to make it very clear that translations in this book are the interpreted meanings of the Quran. The original Quran is in Arabic language and it is collectively agreed within Islamic theology that the translations cannot be called the

Quran, the sacred revelation. Therefore, one should realize this very fine point that this book is not the Quran. Hence, the title, "Selected Passages from the Quran with Interpreted Meanings." It is always encouraged and stipulated in practice and scholarly endeavors to learn the language of Arabic as well as the scriptural sciences to appropriate the meanings of the Quran.

It is interesting to note for the English reader that one of the names or attributes of the Quran mentioned in the Quran itself, is al-Muhaymin or al-Musaddiq. Al-Muhaymin can mean the guardian of the Bible: the New and Old Testaments. This means that the role of the Quran is to ensure and acknowledge that God sent the Gospel to Jesus, Torah to Moses, and Psalms to David. Therefore, the Quran reassures in many of its verses that the the Bible: Psalms, Gospels, and Torah were the revelations from God, Allah. Also, al-Mussadiq is the name of the Quran which can be translated as the Confirming Scripture of the Bible: the New and Old Testaments. The Quran confirms the similar teachings in the Bible: the Gospel, the Psalms, and the Torah especially in the scopes of the belief such as believing in One God, and accountability in the afterlife, and in the scopes of ethical behavior such as the actualization of justice in personal and social levels.

Although there are minimal transliterated words, this book uses a simplified version of the standard academic transliteration for the non-English words. For example, the letter a'yn(ε) in Arabic, is denoted with an apostrophe '. Also, the Arabic elongation letters are mostly not reflected in the transliteration. Rather than using widely accepted academic transliteration protocols, the purpose of these simplifications is to hopefully ensure ease for the unfamiliar reader of Arabic literature. Also, the superscripts with parenthesis refer to the relevant citations and the superscripts without parenthesis refer to footnotes. In this book, at least one verse from each chapter of the Quran is selected to introduce the unfamiliar English reader to the main sacred text of Islam. Instead of using original chapter names as presented above, the selected themes of the verses are used as the titular representations for each chapter. The first number in the brackets denotes the chapter numbers and the second number denotes the verse numbers within the chapter.

1. The Opening

The first chapter of the Quran, "Al-Fatiha" is often translated as "The Opening." Described as the door of the Quran, It is also regarded as the opening of the Quran's meanings. According to the exegetical scholars, the message of the entire Quran is embedded in this short seven-line opening chapter. The in-door opening represents knowing one's internal potential self with the teachings of the Quran. The outdoor opening represents knowing the world and universe with the teachings of the Quran.

The Opening

In the name of God, the All Merciful, the Very Merciful

All praise and all appreciation belongs to *God*.
God, the Originator, the Upholder and the Maintainer[44] of all the universes, heavens and galaxies,[45]
God, the All Merciful, the Very Merciful
God, the only Authority and Decision-Maker of the Day of Accountability.

---

44. Rabb is translated as God with the Arabic context of the Originator, Upholder, and Maintainer in this context. The classical translations [5][6][4][3][2][7] for Rabb in other texts come generally with the word "Lord" except the M. Asad's translation [1]. Language is a constant changing phenomena with time, context, and culture. A word a decade ago may not have the same contextual meaning when used today in our time. The word Lord in classical English can refer to the authority and ownership with slavery with negative embedded meanings [8] in our current time. Also, especially in Christian theology, it is commonly used for Jesus which may cause confusion for the reader. One of the common words in daily usage of this word today is related to the owner of a property referred to as the landlord which can have reductive meanings for the general English reader. Oppositely, in Arabic, Rabb has many meanings such as upbringing, nourishing, teaching, making order, upkeeping, caregiving, controlling, safeguarding, and maintaining with love, mercy, and care. Therefore, the best example of the usage of this word in Arabic can be that when parents have a relationship with their child with all these qualities of the word Rabb with love, mercy, and care. In this text, different attributes and names of God are embedded in the contextual meanings of Rabb. One can realize the similar approach in M. Asad's translation [1]. He uses Sustainer as the translation of Rabb, which is a very good attempt to change the traditional vocabulary for this word, but I think it is not sufficient to include all the meanings of Rabb depending on the context.
45. Alamin is translated as the galaxies which are observable and predictable in astrophysics. The word galaxy is also known and is commonly used. In this text, specific technical and scientific terminologies are avoided if they are not known and used in the everyday language of English. Universe and heaven are inserted to reflect the classical translations for the word of Alamin.

PART 2   Selected Passages from the Quran with Interpreted Meanings

God, You alone, we do worship, and
God, from You alone, we do seek help.

Oh *God*, guide us to the continuous permanent correct and straight path
Oh *God*, to the path of those on whom You have showered Your Grace and Blessings,
Oh *God*, not to the path of those who claim to follow Your guidelines but disrespectful of You,
Oh *God*, not to the path of those who claim to love You but don't follow the true guidelines from You,

Amen.
[1:1–7]

Commentary

According to Islamic scholars, this first chapter of the Quran may be short in length, but it is dense in meaning. Therefore, the chapter is critical in practice. The chapter is repeated in the Muslim daily prayers and some of the scholars think that it embodies the essential meaning of the Quran. In a prophetic narration, there was a person who was sick during the prophet's lifetime. A companion of the Prophet read this seven-line chapter to the sick person and he was cured. The incident was reported to the Prophet. The Prophet smiled and said "The chapter of Opening is a cure."[10]

Some of the scholars explain that God is teaching us how to pray to God in this short chapter as well. The first four lines explain who God is. The second two lines explain the person's mental and spiritual position in prayer. The last four lines are the prayer itself. In other words, in the first lines, God explains the Divine Self. In the second part, the person places his or her position in the relationship with God, and then finally, the person asks from God about one's most important needs in a very condensed form in everyday life.[41]

Discussion Questions

1. Why does the Quran start with this chapter?
2. Why is this chapter read repetitively in daily prayers?

2. This Book

This Book

Alef. Laaaam. Meeeem.[46]

Here[47] is the Noble Book for you,
There is no doubt in it
This Book is Precise, Distinct, True, Real, Clear, Strong, Evident, and Pure
Guidance for *the ones*
who have the attitude of humbleness, love, sincerity and respect for God[48]
The ones who believe in the unseen and mysterious realities beyond the senses as revealed from God[49]
The ones who regularly establish and engage in prayers: physically, mentally, and spiritually[50]
The ones who spend and share what We have given to them from: wealth, knowledge, and kindness
The ones who believe in the Quran, the Bible: Gospel, Psalms, the Torah, and any prior Books from God[51]

---

46. These are the three names of letters in Arabic sounding as A, L, and M in English. No one knows what it means except God according to the exegetical scholars. Although there are some discussions about the possible meanings of these letters, God starts the scripture with some unknown codes to teach humans the attitude of humbleness that there are limits of human knowledge and mind but humility, acceptance, and respect are the key elements in learning and practice.
47. Zalika in Arabic is composed of three letters, "za, lam, and kaf." The word "here" to indicate nearness for the letter "za"; noble indicating distance and highness for the letter "lam"; and the letter "kaf" indicating "a personal book, for you" with the pronoun "ka." Other translations use the word "that" to translate this word to imply respect for far distance which is in Arabic but English does not carry this meaning with the word "that."
48. Muttaqin is translated as the attitude of humbleness, love, sincerity and respect for God.
49. Al-Ghayb is not present which is the unseen and mysterious realities beyond the senses as revealed from God. These are the realities that are beyond the senses and the scope of intellect.
50. Iqama is a word interpreted when used with salah as to be fully concentrated and engaged in the prayer. The expression "regularly establish and engage prayers" is interpreted as minimum requirement of five times daily prayers.
51. For the translation of "unzila ilayka wa min qablika" the normative exegetical interpreted meanings are used.

The ones who believe[52] in the afterlife and the meeting day with God with firm conviction

These are the ones who are on the *Guidance* from their Merciful and Nourishing God,[53] and
These are the ones who for sure will be happy, successful and peaceful.[54]
[2:1–5]

Commentary

The first five verses of the second chapter briefly introduces the Quran as a scripture. It first starts with an opening, explaining who can benefit from this book.[55] The line especially emphasizes the people with taqwa who can benefit most from this scripture. Taqwa can be translated as love, fear, and respect of God. A person of taqwa has the sincere intention of learning and improving oneself. According to the many exegetical[56] scholars, the Reminder, the Quran, has four main themes: understanding the notion of believing in one Creator; establishing the justice and ethical behavior; rationalizing the certainty about afterlife, accountability, and meeting with God; and finally recognizing all these through different means such as the prophets, messengers, and the scriptures. These five verses have these four themes embedded in their meanings.

Discussion Questions

1. What is the meaning of Alef. Laaaam. Meeeem?
2. Why does the Quran require believing in the Bible: the Gospel, the Psalms, and the Torah, not only the Quran itself?
3. Why is there an adjective "with certainty" for the belief of the afterlife but none in other types of beliefs?

---

52. Muqinun is translated as the belief with rational firm conviction due to the word "iyqaan."
53. Rabb is translated as the Merciful and the Nourisher, God according to the context.
54. Muflihun is translated as happy, successful, and peaceful.
55. Hudan lil muttaqin.
56. Exegetical is tafsir in Ar.

God[57]

God, there is no deity except God,
God, the Alive and the Active
God, the Permanent and the Forever

Sleep or unawareness does not touch *God*

Everything on the galaxies[58] belongs to *God*
Everything on the earth belongs to *God*

Who can claim any power next to *God*?
except if God gives permission

God knows everything
secret or public,
internal or external,
past or future.

Who can get anything from *God's* knowledge?
except if God gives permission
God's control[59] surrounds and overpowers everything
the galaxies and the earth.
Who can maintain and uphold their complicated structure in order?[60]
except *God*

After all this, understand!
God is the Magnificent, the Greatest.
[2:255]

---

57. Ayatal Kursi, literally translates as the Throne verse.
58. In the present discoveries of science, galaxies are the biggest human estimated and observable entities that is used in everyday language. Therefore, the word galaxies is preferred as the closest translation for assamawat.
59. Al-Kursi is translated exegetically as the control, dominion, and authority.
60. Hifz is protection, maintenance, and continuity so that there is no chaos and destruction.

Commentary

This is a very critical verse in the Muslim practice. It is the practice of the Prophet to recite this verse after completing each regular daily prayers. This verse has a distinction in practice because it explains about God. Any verse that directly explains about God has a distinct value.

In everyday practice, people especially read this verse for protection purposes. In a famous narration, the Prophet mentions that if a person reads this verse before sleeping, God sends an angel for that person standing outside his door as a guardian for protection until the person wakes up.[26][10]

Discussion Questions

1. Why is sleep (or unawareness) specifically mentioned as a human limitation that is not applicable to God?
2. Is tiredness associated with sleep? How can we conceptualize this association in our relationship with God? Is it an alienating or non-isolating image of God? Why?

The Friend and the Friend

God is the *Friend*[61]
of all believers, recognizers appreciators, and grateful ones
Takes them from the depths of piles of darkness, torture and suffering
To the light, peace, joy, and happiness in this life and after death
all other glorified things[62] except God are *the friends*
of unrecognizers and unappreciators
Take them from light to the spiritual darkness,[63] torture, stress and
    suffering in this life

---

61. Waliyy is translated as the Friend.
62. Tagut is translated as any deity except God. A person's tagut can be anything that person is scared of, or take refuge in, or do an action to please to, except God.
63. In the scripture, darkness is plural which implies different depressive states of human psychology and spirituality according to exegetical scholars.

Then, they become the *friends*[64] of torture and suffering[65] after death
Staying there too long[66]...
[2:257]

Commentary

In Islam, pure belief and total reliance on only God are of paramount importance. Reliance on friends and family can be painful and problematic. Loving friends and family only for the sake of God is a guiding principle of all believers. The love for anything or anyone that is attributed to the love of God is the highest level of relationship with the creation. The real Friend is always God.

Discussion Questions

1. Who is the real Friend according to the Quran?
2. How can earthly friends lead a person to darkness?

Everyone

The prophet believed in the *Revelation*
The believers believed in the *Revelation*

Everyone believed in One, and Only God
Everyone believed in Gabriel, Michael, and all angels
Everyone believed in Bible: the Gospel, the Psalms, and the Torah, and Quran and all the books
Everyone believed in Moses, Jesus, Muhammad as the chosen messengers from God
Everyone believed other messengers and all the prophets chosen by God
There is *no superiority* of one book over another
There is *no superiority* of one prophet over another

---

64. Ashab is translated as the friend.
65. Nar is translated as torture and suffering.
66. Khalidina fiha is translated as staying there too long as one of the minority exegetical interpretations. This choice also optimize the flow and context. The majority of the translations render this expression as "staying there infinitely" due to the majority stance of exegetical interpretations.

PART 2 Selected Passages from the Quran with Interpreted Meanings

And they ended their proclamation as:
> We received the message and surrendered and submitted
> You are Our only, One, the most Merciful God
> We will meet with You soon

[2:285]

Commentary

This verse outlines the pillars of the Muslim belief system. Islam is not a new religion but continuation of the same message of the Gospel revealed to Prophet Jesus, the same message of Torah revealed to Prophet Moses, and the same message of the Quran revealed to Prophet Muhammad. In Islamic creed, for example, if a Muslim says "I don't believe in Jesus or Moses," or "I don't believe in the Bible or Torah," then this person is not considered a Muslim in Islamic theology. To remember this creed, the Prophet Muhammad recommends every Muslim after the night prayer before going to sleep, reading this verse as a reminder and renewal of their inclusive belief.[10]

Discussion Questions

1. Why are these verses important in Islamic theology?
2. Why is it required to believe in the Bible: the Gospel, the Psalms, and the Torah for Muslims?
3. Why is it required to believe in the teachings of Jesus, Moses, and other prophets/messengers sent by God?
4. How is the recitation of these verses practiced in daily life in different Muslim societies?

3. Common Word

Family of Jesus

Alef. Laaaam. Meeeem.

God, there is no deity except God,
God, the Alive and the Active
God, the Permanent and the Forever

God revealed the Book to you
with the truth, certainty and precision
confirming what God already revealed before
The Bible: the Gospel, the Psalms, and the Torah
[3:1–3]

Discussion Question

1. In comparison to the other divine scriptures, what is the status of the Quran in Islam?

Adam and Jesus

With certainty,
The nature of Jesus to God is similar to the nature of Adam
Whom God created Adam from dust and
said: "Be", he was.

The truth is from your Teaching and Upbringing God. Then,
Don't be from the ones who is hesitant and doubtful.
[3:59–60]

Discussion Questions

1. How is the creation of Adam and Jesus similar in Islamic theology?
2. What is the perception of Jesus in Islam?
3. Why is there an assurance against doubt in the above verse?

Common Word

Inform all Christians and Jews and other followers of a scripture about this amazing fact!
Please pay attention followers of the earlier revelations!
Let's get together and realize the values that you and we hold in common!
Among these values, primarily, is:
We worship only to God. We should not worship anything except our same and common Creator.[67]
This is because; we should not ascribe any equal with God.
And therefore, we should not consider human beings as divine.
We believe that only God is divine.
After all, if they reject this message then tell them:
"Be our witness that we submit ourselves to one God"
[3:64]

Discussion Questions

1. What is the understanding of "common" in the verse above?
2. What is the importance of this verse for different interfaith engagements for Muslims, especially in the West?

---

67. The Arabic reader will note that "That we only worship God" is inserted in the translation to give an exegetical complementary meaning to the following part: "We should not worship anything except to our Same and Common Creator."

Rotation of Days

If an evil touched you
Then remember that
Evil touches others as well.

These are the days
We rotate among the people
The days of good and evil
So that the real characters
Of people are revealed
God knows it and
You will be a witness to it as well

Remember!
God does not like oppressors
[3:140]

Discussion Questions

1. How can one understand the "rotation of days" among people?
2. Is it possible to avoid evil and live a life without it? What is the importance of prayers to avoid evil in Islam?

4. Creation in Pairs

Creation in Pairs

Oh People!
Have love, conscience, and respect of God
Who created you from one self and
Created from this self its pair
And spread you on earth as
Men and women

Have fear and respect of God
From Who you always ask your needs.

Have fear and respect of God
Refrain cutting relationships with each other and with your relatives

Remember!
Indeed, God is watching over you.
[4:1].

Commentary

This verse reminds us of the notion of humans as one species, and we are from the same family. Therefore, one should maintain justice and ethical behavior in this understanding of universal brotherhood and sisterhood. It reminds us to have fear and respect for God in order not to go over limits and oppress one another; although people may not realize it but God knows it and there will be accountability after death for each person.

Discussion Question

1. Why are fear and respect for God repeated in the same verse?

Does God oppress?

Indeed and Definitely,
God does not oppress even a little
Even of a size or smaller than an atom.

And, oppositely,
If the person has a small good effort,
God increases its reward in multitude and
Gives this person special and enormous gifts
From the Grace of the Divine.
[4:40]

Discussion Questions

1. What is the relationship between authority and oppression?
2. What are some narratives in our contemporary time for different religions about the concept of authority, God, and oppression?
3. Accordingly, how do you understand this verse?
4. What is the main theological teaching embedded in this verse when God bestows multitude rewards for a single good effort, and yet, no such multiplicity in punishment is accorded to a single evil act?

Pure Belief

Indeed,
God does not forgive a person
if they did not recognize One and Pure Creator before they die

Other than that,
With the Divine will,
God can forgive everyone for all the other wrongs and evil.
[4:48]

Discussion Question

1. Why is unrecognition of One and Pure Creator not forgiven by God according to the theology but everything else can be forgiven with God's mercy?

Don't they think about this Quran?

After all this,
Don't they critically think about this Quran!
If it was from anyone other than God
Definitely, they would find a lot of contradictions.
[4:82]

Discussion Questions

1. How can "critical thinking" help in establishing the authenticity of a divine text?
2. What do the above verses urge the readers while engaged in reading the Quran?

The Etiquette of Greeting

And,
If you are greeted with kind words
Then, greet this person better than her or his greeting

Or,
At least, return the same greeting in the similar way of niceness

Indeed, and definitely remember that,
God accounts for everything.
[4:86]

Discussion Question

1. Why is greeting a person emphasized and important in theology both in the teachings of the scripture and the Prophet Muhammad?

More Truthful Words

There is no deity except Allah
Definitely, God will gather you in the Day of Accountability
There is no doubt about it.

Whose words can be more truthful other than God's?
[4:87]

Discussion Question

1. Why does God emphasize truthfulness of the Divine words in the scripture?

Hiding from Who?

They want to hide from people
And
They don't want to hide from God

But
God is with them
When they are planning the evil
Which God is not pleased of it.

Don't worry!
God surrounds them
With the Divine Knowledge and Power
[4:108]

Discussion Question

1. Can the belief that God's knowledge encompasses all things (and events) restrain an individual from committing an evil deed? Why?

5. Conflict and Justice

Conflict and Justice

Oh you who believe!
Be the ones who are consistent witnesses
In establishing the justice for the sake of God
And don't let the hate or dislike of a group
Deviate you from justice

Be just and fair!
This the closest character of a person who is God conscious
Fear and have respect for God!
God knows what you are doing.
[5:8]

Discussion Question

1. According to the verse above, what is the relationship between fairness and a close relationship with God (in piety)?

The Prophet, the Quran, and the Followers of the Bible: the Gospel, the Psalms, and the Torah and the Educated People

Oh Educated People![68], Christians, and Jews who follow the Bible: the Gospel, the Psalms, and the Torah!
Indeed, Our prophet Muhammad came to you
Explaining to you what has been hidden from the books, the Bible: the Gospel, the Psalms, and the Torah
This Prophet is calling you nicely with forgivenesss

---

68. Ahlu Kitab is translated with the classical exegetical meanings and with a contemporary meaning of a person who may have an education represented with the notions of learning from the books.

Oh Educated People, Christians, and Jews who follow the Bible: the
> Gospel, the Psalms, and the Torah!
Indeed,
a light, the Prophet Muhammad and
a clear book, the Quran
has come to you.

God guides with this Prophet and this Book to the Divine pleasure and
> to the path of peace
Taking them out from the ocean of darkness to the light and peace
> with the will of God and
Guiding them to a continuous and permanent correct and peaceful life.
[5:15–16].

Discussion Questions

1. Why do all the prophets (Prophet Muhammad, Moses, Jesus, etc.) complement one another with similar teachings?
2. What is the status of Prophet Muhammad among the followers of Christianity and Judaism?

6. Ecosystem and Species

Knowing about the Prophet with Certainty

The ones who we gave them scripture such as the Bible: the Gospel, the
     Psalms, and the Torah
Know and recognize the Prophet Muhammad
As if they recognize and know their own children with certainty.
After this,
If they deny this fact, they betray their own moral values
Then,
The ones who betray their own selves are not going to believe.
[6:20]

Discussion Question

1. Why are Christians, Jews, and other Divine bookholders expected to know and recognize the Prophet Muhammad with certainty?

Lying against Their Own Selves

Look at those!
How they lie against their own selves and
Whatever they are making up
Will leave them alone
[6:24]

Discussion Question

1. What is meant by "they lie against their own selves"?

Ecosystem and Species

There is no moving creature on the earth or
Flying with wings in the sky that

They are community and species like yours, humans, in the ecosystem.

We have not left out anything in the book
That ultimately be gathered and returned to God
[6:38]

Discussion Question

1. How does the Quran teach that all creatures have their own community?

Appreciating the Scriptures Revealed by God

They did not appreciate God with a true appreciation[69] when they said:
God did not reveal anything to any human being
Then, ask them:
Who revealed the book, the Torah, that came to Moses?
And this book was a clear light and guidance for the people.

They were putting some of this book on pages but
They were hiding most of it.

On the other hand,
In this Quran, you are taught about a knowledge
Neither you nor your fathers[70] knew before.

---

69. This appreciation can change depending on the societies and time. For example, the initial Meccan pagans did know God but at the same time they worshipped other idols. This was not the true appreciation of God. The people of the scriptures such as Christians or Jews had changes in the original teachings of their creed and theology that were brought by their messengers/prophets such as Jesus or Moses. Some of them followed these false teachings. This was not the true appreciation of God. The Muslims had the authentic teachings of God with the Quran and with the teachings of the Prophet Muhammad. Yet, some of them did not apply these teachings fully in their practice. This was not the true appreciation of God.
70. Fathers can denote the knowledge transferred from cultures.

If still they don't accept it.
Just tell them:
Definitely, God revealed this book, the Quran.
If still they don't accept it, then
Leave them in their own occupation in a self-deceptive game.
[6:91]

Discussion Question

1. In comparison to the Bible: the Gospel, the Psalms, and the Torah, what is the status of the Quran in Islam?

7. Doing the evil and blaming others?

Doing the evil and blaming others?

And when they do evil they say:
"Indeed, we have inherited this act from our culture[71] and society
And also, God ordered us to do this."
Tell them:
Definitely, God does not order doing any evil!
Are you making up something about God that really you don't know?

Tell them:
My Upbringing and Just God always orders the good, the ethical, the fair and the just.
And pray and turn to God in all worship places
Call God with sincerity, only believing and trusting in One!
That is the due of the religion only for God
And remember!
As you were nothing, you were created in the beginning
You will return to God at the end.
[7:28–29]

Discussion Questions

1. How is the psychology of blaming others when there is an evil?
2. Why do people blindly follow or disregard a culture or social norm?
3. How do you compare following a religion or a belief in a culture compared to ethical values? Are they similar or different? Why?

---

71. Abaana is translated as "culture and society" instead of forefathers or fathers as translated in other translations. Current, more popular usage of inheriting a habit and doing it as a norm is named as culture and social values as Tylor states. (***Popular Science Monthly* 26 (1884): 145. Public Domain.)**

8. Uniting the Hearts

Uniting the Hearts

And,
God united their hearts.
If you spent all the wealth and resources on the earth
You were not able to unite their hearts.
But only God united them.
Definitely, God is the High, the Exalted, and the source of Wisdom.
[8:63]

Discussion Question

1. How can an individual implement the above teaching in everyday life when a conflict occurs?

9. Trade

Trade

God bought from the believers their body and wealth
With the repayment of Heaven.
[9:111]

Commentary

According to Islam, *the body, good health, time, physical and mindful strength, opportunities, strength, wealth, etc.* are bestowed by God for the person to use and invest in good deeds. Scholars have referred to these gifts from God as "advanced payments" and tools that are to be exploited for the greater good.

Although the person does not really own him or herself, it is granted by God on the earth as a trust [33:72] as if the person has the full ownership and control over oneself. This is due to the God-given free will of the person.

It is expected to make good investments with these tools. These investments are not forced but the person has the free will to choose evil or good. Therefore, in the Quran, this notion of business with God is presented. Islamic teachings encourage the middle way in both worldly and spiritual matters as the person has bodily and spiritual needs.

Discussion Question

1. How is the relationship between the person and God symbolized as a trade in the above verse?

Categories

Give good news to the believers!
The ones who try to always seek repentance from *God*
The ones who try to always worship *God*
The ones who try to always be grateful to *God*
The ones who try to always travel for the sake of *God*
The ones who try to always bow and prostrate to God in their prayer
The ones who try to always encourage the good and prevent evil and bad things
The ones who try to always observe the limits set by *God*.
[9:112]

Discussion Question

1. How do you understand different categorization of people in their relationship with God?

10. Will you force people to believe?

Will you force people to believe?

And
If your Merciful, Just, and Caregiving God wanted
Definitely, everyone on the earth will believe in God
After this,
Are you going to force people to believe in God?
[10:99]

Discussion Questions

1. Is belief a choice in theology? How and why?
2. Does the Quran teach forcing people to believe?
3. How can one explain the narratives about "forced conversions" of the expansion of Islam in some of the historical narratives?

Alternation of Night and Day

Surely, in the alternation of night and day and
In what God has created in the skies, galaxies and the universe and the earth,
There are signs for people who are God conscious.

As for those who do not believe in meeting with Us and
are quite happy with the life of this world and
are content with it,
then those are the ones who are neglectful of Our signs.
[10:6–7]

Discussion Question

1. What is a sign according to the Quran?

11. Continuous Struggle

Continuous Struggle

After all this,
Struggle constantly
To be on the straight and correct path
As you are instructed
With the ones who turn to God

Do not oppress and pass the limits!

Definitely and Surely,
God sees and is aware of
With what you are constantly preoccupied.
[11:112]

Discussion Questions

1. Is it difficult to constantly struggle for spiritual cleansing? Why?
2. What is important for theology: the effort of struggle or the ultimate result of the struggle as failure or achievement? Why?

12. Language of the Revelation

The first verse and the first word revealed to the Prophet Muhammad from God was to "Read." It meant to read, learn, and think on all the signs of God. The verse is written in Arabic in a style of calligraphy.

Language of the Revelation

Alif. Laaaam. Ra.

These are the verses of the clear Book.

For sure and definitely,
We revealed the Quran
In the language of Arabic,
So that there is no confusion
of originality and authenticity
That you can use your mind and intellect.[72]
[12:1–2]

Discussion Question

1. Why is the language of the revelation as Arabic specifically mentioned in the Quran itself?

---

72. Arabic language has a mathematical structure. A person can derive other words from the same word if one knows the rules of derivation. Therefore, non-Arabs can learn this language at any age easily and even speak without an accent with proper eloquent Arabic better than a native speaker. It is interesting to note that only 10% (~200 million) of the Muslim population is native Arabs and the rest are non-Arabs (~1.8 billion).

The Best Story

We tell you
The best story of all
From what we have revealed
In this Quran,

And, indeed,
You were not informed,
Before.
[12:3]

Commentary

The best story mentioned above is the story of Joseph, the son of Jacob, mentioned in detail in the Quran. The story has a variety of appeals, motifs, and themes: linguistic eloquence of the full story, notions of wisdom, patience, unexpected events, always reliance on God, and opportunistic theories. One can interestingly relate this to the contemporary themes of the movie-making industry with the notions of power (position), love, religion, imprisonment, parents, jealousy, hatred, women, game theory, and dreams. It is interesting to note also that a lot of people who became Muslim tend to choose the name of Joseph (Yusuf) due to this story explained in the Quran.

Discussion Question

1. Why is this story deemed to be the best in the Quran?

13. Moving the Mountains, Splitting the Earth, and Speaking with the Dead

Moving the Mountains, Splitting the Earth, and Speaking with the Dead

If there is a book that
the mountains are moved, or
the earth is destroyed, or
the dead is made to speak

Then, definitely it would have been
This Book, the Quran.
[13:31]

Discussion Questions

1. What makes the Quran so important in theology and practice?
2. What are some possible talismanic usages of the Quran in practice?

14. A Nice Word and a Nice Tree

A Simple Good Word and a Nice, Strong Tree

Don't you see
How God brings the example
Of a simple good and pleasant word
Similar to a nice tree:

Its roots are very strong and
Its branches are in the sky.
[14:24]

Discussion Questions

1. How can a good word be similar to a nice tree?
2. What is the relationship between a tree *(with strong roots and high branches)* and *a good word*?

15. Upgraded and Downgrade

I Wish

Alif. Laaaam. Ra.
These are the verses of the Book,
The clear Quran.

Many will wish from the ungrateful ones,
I wish I followed the true and correct way of God and be in peace.[73]
[15:1-2]

Discussion Question

1. Why is the importance of following the true and correct way of God emphasized so much in the Quran?

Upgraded and Downgraded

We know who are upgraded constantly
We know who are downgraded constantly
[15:24]

Commentary

There is a notion of daily struggle in advancing the spiritual relationship on the path of God. One can make a resemblance of the bull and bear markets in the stock market, for example. A prime example of the downgrade is Satan when he was at the highest level then he becomes at the lowest in his closeness to God. Therefore, in practice, as long as the person is alive, the person can spiritually excel or lose depending on the struggle, intention, and sincerity. No one knows their true spiritual state until the person meets with God. Although the time of death is unknown, a sinner can become very pious and a pious person can become an evil person in their journey of life before they die. The

---

73. Muslim is translated as not as a group phenomenon but means following "true way of God." The same word is used for Abraham as a Muslim although he was historically long before the religion of Islam.

spiritual state of the person right before death is very critical because the person will meet God in this state. According to the theology, this final spiritual state of the person will determine the final and permanent abode of the person in afterlife. Due to the uncertainty of the time of death, each person is expected to be watchful of his/her moral and piety states with people and God.

Discussion Question

1. How can the uncertainty of gaining or losing on the spiritual path affect a person in his/her struggle?

16. Bee

Milk, Blood, and Excretion

And, for sure, there is a lesson for you in cattle, sheep, goats....
We feed you from their bellies.
A pure and pleasant milk comes miraculously
From a place between
Blood and excretion meet.
[16:66]

Bee

And,
your Merciful, Upbringing, and Caregiving God inspired to the bee
to take homes on mountains, trees, and hives.
[16:68]

Commentary

The Quran constantly urges the reader to think about different beings on the earth and how they benefit the humans.

Discussion Questions

1. How can one view daily routines or incidents as something normal or abnormal?
2. What are the two different approaches or questions that religion, Islam, and science are seeking to answer for the living and non-living things? Are science and religion complementary in Islam?

Things Other Than God

And,
What they worship other than God,
Cannot create anything.
They are themselves created.
[16:20]

Discussion Question

1. Why does the Quran constantly challenge the false deities for their inability to create and give life?

Two gods?

And God said:
Don't adopt two gods,
Don't adopt two deities, or
Don't adopt anything that is overpowering you other than God
For sure, your Creator, God is only One.

Therefore, to Me stand alone in awe!
[16:51]

Commentary

In Islamic theology, God is the Creator: *Good and evil, ugly and beautiful, believers and non-believers,* etc. Every creation has a purpose. God permits humans use of their free will in decision-making. However, this permission does not imply that God is passive and has left humans to their own devices after creation. Rather, there is a continuous intervention in nature and in God's creations. In a person's life, God's intervention can be very obvious and clear, and yet for some, it can be mystical and esoteric.

There is no duality in understanding who the Creator is. God is only One. In external guidelines of theology, although a person can verbally accept this notion of surrendering oneself to One and only God, in practice, a spiritual journey exists to perfect the understanding of this notion internally. In other words, if a person is scared of anything other than God, this perspective of duality of two deities may still exist. The goal of spiritual purification is a lifelong struggle aimed at fully turning to only one God.

Discussion Questions

1. Is it easy or difficult to discharge oneself from all worries except God? Why?
2. How can it help the person if the person does not have any real worries except the relationship with God?

Ethical Behavior

Certainly,
God orders justice, fairness, and
Niceness, good conduct, and
Generosity towards one's fellow-men.

And forbids
Immorality and unethical behavior,
Evil,
Oppression.

God is giving you advice.
So that, perhaps, you indeed take this advice and think about it.
[16:90]

Discussion Questions

1. According to the above verse, what is good and what is evil?
2. What is the significance of the above verse in Friday sermons for Muslims?

17. Beautiful Names of God

Doing Good

If you do good it is for your own benefit
If you do something bad it is against your own self
[17:7]

Discussion Questions

1. How is this verse understood in practice?
2. Is the understanding of "karma" similar to the teaching of this verse?

Calling Evil as Good

And the person calls and wants the evil
As if he or she calls and wants the good
The nature of the human is always hasty
[17:11]

Discussion Question

1. How can a person want the evil assuming that it is good?

The Levels of People

Look!
How we make some people above others
Remember!
The levels in the afterlife will be better and higher than this!
[17:21]

Discussion Questions

1. Are the levels in the above verse related to the spiritual or worldly levels?
2. Are the levels in this world related to the levels in the afterlife? For example, if someone is rich, is this person considered blessed or spiritually higher than a poor person according to Islam?

Chanting and Glorification of God by All the Beings

All the seven skies and galaxies and earth and between them
Praise, glorify and chant for God

There is nothing left out from all the beings except they perform
The Praise, glorification and chant for their Merciful Creator

But you don't understand their chants
Remember your God is always Caring, Gentle and Forgiving.
[17:44]

Discussion Question

1. Are there people who understand and hear the glorifications of other beings?

The Character of the Person

And when we give something good to the person
This person turns away from God and does not care.

When an evil hits this person
She or he becomes hopeless

Tell them:
Everyone shows and acts according to their own character
Therefore, your Watchful and Merciful God knows who is better on the
    path.
[17:84–85]

Discussion Question

1. Do the humans naturally tend to appreciate good? Why?

Challenge to All Creation about the Quran

Tell this challenge to them:
If all the humans and Jinns (other beings)[74] come together
To put together a Quran similar to this one
For sure, they will not be able to bring a similar one
Even if they support each other fully on this task
[17:88]

Discussion Questions

1. How is this challenge understood in practice? What is the essence of this challenge?
2. How can the order "tell them" be interpreted in the above verse? Who is giving this order?

What prevents a person from believing and accepting?

And what prevents people from believing
When the guidance come to them is due to
Their only statement:
"Does God send a human as a messenger?"

Tell them:
If on the earth lived angels instead of humans
Then, we would send them an angel as a messenger

Therefore, tell them:
God is sufficient as a witness between me and you
Indeed, God is always the Knower and the Seer of the true state
Of all God's creation
[17:94]

Discussion Questions

1. Why do the humans expect a non-human messenger from God? What is their reason or rationale?
2. How is the response to this expectation in the above verse?

---

74. Jinn is translated as non-humans for the English reader.

The Beautiful Names of God

Say:
You call your Creator as Allah or the Most Merciful, Ar-Rahman
It doesn't matter!

Whatever name you call your Merciful God with
Definitely, your Creator has all the beautiful names

And when you communicate with your Hearing and Seeing God in
    your prayers
You don't need to raise your voice or whisper
Be natural, be in between and follow the middle way
[17:110]

Discussion Questions

1. According to the theology, what is the significance of calling and knowing God with the beautiful names?
2. Which one is more important, having knowledge about God with correct understanding or referring to God with the special or proper names in the scriptures? Why?

18. Appreciating the Book

Arabic Calligraphy of AL HAMDU LILLAHI, which means all true appreciation is for God only. There are chapters of the Quran which start with this expression. This chapter starts with the appreciation of and thanking God about the revelation of the Quran. This expression is written in Arabic calligraphy in the above picture.

Appreciation for the Book

Thanks and all appreciation to God that
God revealed the book for the person who recognizes and appreciates God[75]
And this book does not have any mistake or error in it,
Is fully perfect.

Discussion Questions

1. Why should there be an appreciation when God communicates with the creation through a formal scripture?
2. How can someone's attitude be with the Book who recognizes and appreciates God compared to its opposite?
3. Why is it emphasized that this Book is perfect and that there are no errors or mistakes therein?

---

75. Although, the book is revealed to the Prophet to convey to other humans. The notion of personalization is important in theology as if the scripture is an individual revelation to each person to directly communicate with God without any intermediator.

19. Do you hear anything from the dead?

Baby Jesus talks in the Cradle

Then, Mary pointed to Jesus.
People said:
How can we talk to a baby in the cradle?
Baby Jesus said:
"I am the servant and creation of God.
God gave me the Book and
Made me a prophet and messenger."
[19:29–30]

Commentary

According to the above verse, people did not understand how Mary had delivered a baby and they were shocked. Mary at that point exercised her right to silence, kept mute, but pointed to Jesus. Then, as a miracle from God, baby Jesus in the cradle talked to absolve Mary of any unchastity.

Discussion Questions

1. How can one understand baby Jesus's talking in the cradle in theology?
2. How is the understanding of Jesus in Islam according to the above verse?

Do you hear anything from the dead?

And,
We terminated before them many generations.
Do you feel, see or hear even a whisper from the dead or past nations?
[19:98]

Discussion Question

1. What does the above verse imply about the reality of death and communication with death?

20. Is the Quran for difficulty?

Taha

Ta ha.
We did not reveal the Quran to you
so that you have difficulty
But as a reminder for the one
who is humble
[20:1–3]

Discussion Questions

1. What is the purpose of a divine scripture?
2. Why does the verse mention that adherence to a scripture's teachings might be difficult for some people?
3. Why does the verse mention that the Quran was not revealed to impose difficulty?
4. How does the state of being humble affect learning?
5. What is the meaning of Taha in popular practice?

21. The Manual of a Person

The Manual of a Person

For sure and certainly,
We revealed you a book.
Inside, you, yourself is explained
It is talking about you[76]
Don't you understand?
[21:10]

Discussion Question

1. Is the Quran a manual for a person?

---

76. Addition of a sentence, due to the contextual meaning.

22. Creation Process

Creation Process

Oh People!
If you have doubt about recreation after death,

Then, remember!

We created you from the elements on the earth.
In a specific process of sperm and an egg
Then, an embryo,
Then, a growing being with its flesh, and bones but still incomplete,

Keep in mind, we are explaining some of the details of the creation process

Then, we keep this being dwelling and developing in the womb
Until a designated time We want…

Finally, this being comes out as a baby so that it can gain some power

After all, some of you die early some die later

So that everyone completes the journey of knowing and experience

Another creation example is from what you see every day in the garden, on the earth
It looks like there is no plant, but it is dead.
As soon as we send rain on it
It gets alive, starts growing, and becomes green
Such a nice looking flowers, roses, fruits…

After all these examples,

Don't doubt about God

God is Real and the Truth
God creates from nothing
God recreates from death
God is all Powerful.

There is no doubt,
That the meeting time with God is close
God will recreate all the death from graves and from anywhere, doesn't matter

After all this, don't bring arguments
without any knowledge,
without any education,
without any authentic reference
[22:5–8]

Discussion Questions

1. What is the Quranic explanation of the stages in the development of a human embryo?
2. What are the possible reasons behind providing specific details of human embryonic stages in the Quran?
3. How does the Quran relate the details of embryonic development to the recreation after death?

23. The Purpose

Purpose

Do you think that
You were created for nothing, for no purpose?

And,
Do you think that
You will not be returned to Us?

After this,
God is the Ultimate True Authority.
There is no deity except God,
God is the Merciful Sustainer and Owner of the Great and Noble
    Authority, Arshul Karim.[77]
[23:115–116]

Discussion Question

1. According to the Quran, what is the primary purpose of human existence?

Power struggle?

Then the aristocrats and the upper class of the unappreciators from his people said: What is going on!

"This person is a human like you.

He just wants power.

And even,
If really God wanted to send a messenger or prophet
Then it would be an angel instead of a human,

---

77. Merciful Sustainer and Owner is for the word Rabb. Please see the discussion about the translation of the word "Rabb" in Surah Fatiha. Arshul Karim as Great and Noble Authority.

A human messenger is really a weird concept
We haven't heard or seen this type of teaching in our present and
   previous culture, forefathers or society.[78]
[23:24]

Commentary

The above story is an extract of a dialogue between Prophet Noah and his community. While calling his people to believe in the One and only Creator, his community rejected his teachings and attributed his message to a quest for power.

Discussion Question

1. According to the verse above, what are the reasons Prophet Noah's people rejected his teachings?

---

78. Here, "abainaal awwaliin" is translated as "previous culture, forefathers and society" due to contemporary contextualization of this phrase.

24. Walking on Belly and Feet

Walking on Belly and Feet

And,
God created all the moving creatures from water.

Then,
Some move and crawl on their belly and

Some walk on their two feet

Some walk on their four feet.

God creates how ever God wants.

Definitely and for sure,

God has the power to do anything.
[24:45]

Discussion Question

1. How does the Quran depict a person's ability to ponder and reflect by referencing motion on the belly and the feet?

25. Shadow and Change

Shadow and Change

Have you not observed how your All Knower and Merciful God
   stretched out the shadow (of the sun)?
If God so willed, God would have made it stand still.
But, We made the sun an indicator for it.
[25:45]

Commentary

The concept of change is mentioned in different contexts within the Quran. Muslims are encouraged to take advantage of the cyclical nature of time to connect with their Creator. The Quran encourages people to engage themselves in the remembrance of God through devotional acts, rituals, or prayers at all times, especially before/after sunset and sunrise.

Discussion Questions

1. How can external change affect the spiritual state of heart and mind?
2. How can the shadows of objects inspire a relationship with the Divine?

Arrogance as a sign of ungratefulness or Prostration as a sign of respect?

And they were advised
To prostrate as a sign of respect of God, the Most Merciful

They said:
"Who is the Most Merciful?
Do you really think we would respect and prostrate to what you tell
   us?"

And,
This attitude of arrogance in reality increased their hate.
[25:60]

Commentary

The above verse is recognized as a verse of prostration. There are fourteen of such verses in the Quran and some of them show the intrinsic tendencies of humans towards arrogance. When the Prophet read the above verse, he prostrated to glorify the Creator. Hence, when Muslims read any of the verses of prostration, they are obliged to engage in prostration to the Creator. Prostration is understood as an act of awe, respect, and humility towards God. By performing the act of prostration, the believers absolve themselves of the arrogant peoples' actions.

Discussion Question

1. Why do the people give negative responses if they are called to recognize and be respectful to God, the Most Merciful?

26. The Poets and Magicians

The Poets and Magicians

Ta. Seeen. Meeeem.
These are the verses of a clear Book.
You will almost destroy yourself due to to grief because
They don't appreciate and recognize God.

We appreciate your genuine and deep concern but don't Worry!

If We wanted we could have brought to them the signs
Which would have forced them to be humble and appreciative.
And,
When they had a new reminder from the Most Merciful, God
Their attitude was only to say "I don't care"

For sure,
They are denying it but
Soon, they will have the news and the results of
What they have been denying, and not caring.
[26:1–6]

Discussion Questions

1. Does God appreciate and reward people who are concerned about helping others to establish a relationship with God?
2. How can one understand the above verses for the responsibility of the Prophet Muhammad's invitation?

The Poets and Magicians

Faalqaw hibaalahum wa i'siyyahum
wa qaaluu bi i'zzati fira'wna innaa la nahnul gaalibuun
Faalqa Musa Asahu
Fa itha hiya talqafu ma Ya'fikuun
[26:44–47]

Commentary

The above verse is an example of how the sounds of the Quran, the selection of words, and the overall meaning depicts a scene. These words with different conjugations are underlined and colored above. The context of the above verses is related to the magicians' practice of their craft with tools such as ropes and other items. The selected words in Arabic language portrays this very vivid act of both magicians and Moses' response. The etymological meaning of the words used in the verses implies the delusional effects conjured by magicians with their tools. Whether in medieval Europe, fifth-century Arabia or in other similar cultures, the evil practice of magic has often involved the use of strings and other odd-shaped items with extreme geometries. Along with other litanies and practices of Prophet Muhammed, these verses and other verses in the Quran can be used as an antidote to counter the evil effects of magic or poetry.

Discussion Questions

1. How can one rationalize the importance of reading a divine scripture in its original language of revelation?
2. What is the understanding of magic and poetry in Islam?

27. God from the Bird's Eye

God from the Bird's Eye

The bird said:
"During my travel,
I have found a queen and her people prostrating and worshipping themselves to the sun, instead of God, and the Satan has falsely beautified their actions for them, and therefore
prevented them from the right way, so they do not choose the guidance
I really don't understand!
Shouldn't they prostrate and worship God who brings forth what is hidden in the heavens and the earth, and
Shouldn't they prostrate and worship God who knows whatever you hide and whatever you do in public.
Allah! There is no god but Allah, the Merciful Owner of the Great Authority and Control."[79]
[27:24–26]

Commentary

As mentioned in the previous part of the verse, the bird gets into a very intellectual and rational argument with the Prophet Solomon. The conversation is about a country that the bird found in its excursion. From the character of the bird, it shows that the bird has a clear and definite belief of one Creator. It gives examples in its conversation with Solomon about the majesty of God and how God creates. The bird first cannot rationalize the people worshipping the sun as the Creator as the verse reads as above. Later, the bird mentions that their irrational belief could be due to Satan's misguidance. Satan can show something false as true by using different deceitful beautification or ornamentation methods. Lastly, the bird engages with a real intense theological argument of understanding the divinity and the Creator in the Quran.

---

79. Arsh is translated as Great Authority and Control.

PART 2 Selected Passages from the Quran with Interpreted Meanings

Discussion Questions

1. What is the understanding of animals, plants, and objects in their relationship with God in Islam?
2. How does the bird rationalize the understanding of God in the above verse?

28. Choice of Religion and Fear of Losing Wealth

Choosing a Religion and Fear of Losing the Wealth

And they said:
"If we follow the guidance that is with you then
We will be forced to leave our land and belongings"

If that is the case then, then ask them:

Didn't We place them in a secure and safe country
Where all different types of fruits of wealth are pouring
As a favor from Us?

And, but still
Most of them are making excuses and unaware of this truth
[28:57]

Discussion Questions

1. What are the factors that prevent people from following a religion even though they may agree with its teachings?
2. Are we living in a secure and safe country to make our own choices about religion? Why?
3. From the above verse, who are those expressing a loss of their wealth if they become Muslims?

29. Struggle

Trials and Struggle

Alif, Laam, Meem.
Do the people think that they will be left alone by simply saying that
"We believed in this true faith" and but after this proclaim, they will
   not be tested?
Yes, Indeed.

We have certainly tested those before them, and
God will surely make evident those who are truthful, and
Will surely make evident the untruthful.

Do those who do evil deeds think that they can escape from Us?
What a bad judgment!
Evil is what they base on everything.

Whoever looks forward meeting with God,
Indeed, the scheduled time set by God is definitely approaching.
And God is the All-Hearing, the All-Knowing.

And whoever puts an effort does so only for her or his own good.
Indeed, God does not need anything and anyone;
Definitely, God is independent from all of the worlds, all of the
   creation.
[29:1–6]

Commentary

The verses focus on the concept of fear as part of the Divine way of testing people.

Discussion Question

1. How does one understand the tests, trials, and struggle in life and meeting with God after death?

Struggle

And,

The ones who struggle on Our paths
For sure, We will guide them to Our paths

Definitely and for sure,
God is certainly with the good, humble, forgiving and generous ones.
[29:69]

Commentary

This verse is about tazkiya. Tazkiya is the process of improving oneself and one's relationship with God. In the beginning of this process, the spiritual traveler may subscribe to fear of punishment or hope of reward from God. In later stages, as the person advances through worship, good action, and knowledge in his/her relationship with God, then the person fears losing the love and pleasure of God. Whatever his/her situation, as long as God is happy and pleased with this person, he/she is satisfied and expresses ultimate love and gratitude towards God. An example of a person who fully implemented tazkiya during his entire life was the Prophet Muhammad. He was always in a state of gratitude and thankfulness to God in all situations. The name Muhammad literally translates as "the one who embodied gratitude and thankfulness" in Arabic language.

Discussion Questions

1. What is the importance of struggle in personal spiritual advancement in the relationship with Allah in Islam?
2. What is the most important: the struggle or the result of the struggle?

Experts of the Disciplines and Understanding the Quran

And these examples that we give for the people and
They don't truly understand their true meanings except the experts and specialists
[29:43]

Discussion Question

1. What is the understanding of experts in the above verse? Are they only religious experts or other experts in different fields such as natural sciences?

30. Calmness with Your Spouse

Calmness with Your Spouse

And, it is from God's signs to create you from the elements on the earth
Then, you spread on the earth as humans.

And, it is from God's signs to create for you your spouses from yourself
So that you can find calmness and peace with your spouse and
God made between you and your spouse love and mercy
Indeed, there are signs for the people who think and ponder on all these facts.
[30:20–21]

Discussion Question

1. What is the purpose of marriage according to the above verse?

Effect of Human's Mischief on Land and Sea

Pollution and mischief have appeared on land and sea because of what humans have been doing,
For sure, God makes them taste the results of their action,
So that they may stop and return to the right way.
[30:41]

Commentary

Some of the scholars explain that environmental pollution occurs due to the internal pollution of the mind and heart because of adopting unethical behavior. One of the basic premises of Islam is respecting everything, the nature and all human beings, due to respect to the Divine. If this is not present, then there is internal and ethical pollution. Therefore, external pollution becomes inevitable.

Discussion Question

1. According to the Quran, how do the unethical actions of humans affect the environment?

Cycle of Weakness and Strength in a Person's Life

God is the One
Who created you as a baby, being weak physically and mentally

God is the One
Who made you strong physically and mentally in your youth after this weakness

Then,
God is the One
Who made you physically and mentally weak again in your old age after this strength

Certainly,
God is the All Knower, All Powerful.
[30:54]

Discussion Question

1. How can one understand and interpret this cycle of weakness and strength in one's life?

31. Child Education

Child Education

Oh my Child!
If there is something hidden in the size of a mustard seed, or size of an atom or less than that
On a rock,
In the skies,
In the space, or
On the earth,
God can reveal it and bring it forth.

Certainly, for sure
God is the Gentle, the All Knower.
[31:16]

Commentary

Above is a verse about Prophet Luqman advising his son. Readers should note that there is a disagreement among the Islamic scholars on the status of Luqman as a prophet: While some believe he was only a man of wisdom and piety, others contend that he was indeed a prophet. Luqman admonishes that God's knowledge encompasses all things, including those done in secret. This realization of the Creator's knowledge should compel an individual to avoid evil and engage in good deeds to please God. At the same time, God is the Gentle and always overlooks shortcomings as long as the perpetrator acknowledges his misdeed(s), regrets his action(s), and turns to God in repentance.

Discussion Question

1. How can the above verse have a critical stance on the importance of child education?

Self-Accountability

Oh humans!
Have respect, fear and love for God!

Oh humans!
Prepare yourself for the Day with fear and concern,

In this Day,
Parents cannot help and save their child

In this Day,
The children cannot help and save their parents

Certainly,
The promise and pledge of God is true.

Therefore,
Make Sure!
Don't let this life deceive you.
and
Make Sure!
Don't let the distractions of life and evil doers take you away from God.
[31:33]

Discussion Questions

1. How does this verse emphasize the teaching of self-accountability before God?
2. How does having a pious or evil child affect an individual before God?

32. The Disputes and the Day of Judgment

The Disputes and the Day of Judgment

Definitely,

Your Merciful and Just God

Will pass judgment on the Day of Resurrection and Accountability

About the issues that they have been arguing and disputing.
[32:25]

Discussion Questions

1. What is the importance of believing in afterlife and accountability after death in Islam?
2. Is this belief similar in other religions?

33. Abuse of the Wife

Two Things in One Heart or Two Hearts in One Person

God has not made for any person two hearts in one's chest cavity. [33:4]

Commentary

According to the above verse, it is important to empty everything from the heart and put there only One Being, the Divine. In other words, the heart can and should only have Allah. If someone puts another being in the heart, that heart can become dysfunctional according to the theology. Therefore, the chants, such as "La ilaha illa Allah, there is no deity except God," constantly represent this notion of emptying and filling, because every moment a thought or a feeling enters into one's heart. If there is no effort of cleaning the heart, it will eventually die.

Discussion Question

1. What are the methods of cleansing the heart in Islam?

Differentiating the Role of Wife and Mother

God did not make your wife to be your mother
When using a word of abuse, zihar, to your wife.
[33:4]

Commentary

Although both the mother and wife play vital roles in a man's life, Islam distinguishes the roles of these two important females. This verse orders an end to verbal abuse suffered by wives in the hands of their husbands as practiced in pre-Islamic Arabia. The practice involved the use of the word "zihar" by husbands to describe their wives. In brief, the word conjures up an analogy between the wife and mother's body parts, thus making the wife unlawful to her husband. This unfortunate practice was used to humiliate women and initiate divorce proceedings.

Discussion Questions

1. In our modern world, is it common for men to expect similar roles for their wives and mothers?
2. How can one understand the caretaker role of a woman as a wife compared to a mother in traditional societies?
3. What is the context of the above verse?
4. According to the context of the above verse, how can one consider the desire of a man to divorce his wife because she became old and physically unattractive? Is it considered an abuse?

34. Truth and Attitude

Truth and Attitude

Say:

The truth came and after this
The falsehood cannot bring anything new
Nor it can bring anything from the past.

Say:
If I am on a wrong path
Then, definitely,
I only misguide myself to hurt myself.

If I am on guidance
Then, this will be only possible

By the virtue of what my Merciful God reveals to me.
Certainly,
My Gentle and Caring God is all hearing and very near.
[34:49-50]

Commentary

The above verse is calling people to change their attitude; to learn, listen, and benefit their own selves.

Discussion Questions

1. What is the genuine understanding of the truth and falsehood for a person?
2. What makes a person change his own thinking, belief, attitude, and way of life?
3. According to the Quran, how can the above questions be understood?

35. Evil and its Outcome

If God makes the humans immediately accountable
For what they do,
Then, justice would demand that no human should survive on earth
But the Merciful and Forgiving God
Delays it to a time
When the time comes
God is watching over all of the creation.
[35:45]

Commentary

According to the above verses, God grants all humans a window of opportunity to address a misconduct or shortcoming. In Islam, one of God's attributes is *"The Most Forbearing."* In the scripture, this appellate is generally used along with another attribute of God, *"The Most Forgiving."* Both attributes indicate that the Creator is tolerant, lenient, and patient towards humans. This realization can motivate wrongdoers to reflect on their actions and seek repentance. Then, God, *"The Forgiver,"* overlooks their shortcomings and expunges these misconducts from the record of their deeds.

Discussion Questions

1. How does God respond to the occurrence of evil according to the above verse? Why?
2. Why is there a postponement of accountability when one does an evil action?

36. Embryo and the Enemy

Embryo and the Enemy

Is the person, then, not aware that it is We who create him or her out of
    a simple embryo?
After all these favors,
This person sees Us as a blatant adversary? Is this fair?

Then the same person continues and,
Throws an example and forgets his own creation, says:
Who can give the bones their life after they crumble on the earth after
    death?

Don't Worry,
Tell them nicely:
The One who built and gave life to them before will give life again.
The One, God, is Aware, Knower, and Originator of all types of
    creation.
[36:77–79]

Commentary

Above is one of the famous chapters, yasin, in the Reminder,[80] the Quran. It is common for Muslims to read this chapter every day. This chapter is known and practiced to bring light to the graves of the deceased loved ones. Therefore, when a person visits a cemetery, a Muslim can read this chapter over the buried person.

Discussion Question

1. How does the Quran portray the logic and attitude of a person in the above verse?

---

80. The Quran has a multitude of names and attributes referred by itself in the scripture. One of them is the Dhikr, the Reminder.

37. Removing the Misunderstandings about God

Removing the Misunderstandings about God

Pure and High is Your God,
From how they wrongly describe the Divine.
The One
Who is Perfect,
Free from all false understandings and imaginations of humans.

Therefore,
Constantly, Glorify, Purify, and Correct your thoughts and feelings
    about your Creator
With the Chants and Prayers.

Therefore,
All the Peace, Blessings and Calmness are due for the sincere callers,
    messengers and prophets
For teaching the true and correct understanding of your Creator

Therefore,
Eventually and all the time,
All the Praise, Appreciation and Thanks are only truly for God[81]
Who is the nourisher of all the universes, heavens and galaxies.[82]
[37:180–182]

Commentary

The above lines detach and remove all the misunderstandings about God. In the tradition of recitation of the Quran, the reciters end their reading generally with this line to emphasize the correct understanding of God in theology.

Discussion Question

1. Why is it so critical and important to have the correct understanding of God in Islam?

---

81. Alhamdulillah is translated with the contextual meanings.
82. Rabbul Alamin is translated with the contextual meanings.

38. Satan and His Mission

Critical Thinking on the Quran

The Book
That we revealed to you.
Is
A Light
A source of blessing

So that for sure,
One can ponder,
Reflect and
Think on its verses

So that, for sure
It can be a full reminder
For the smart and intelligent ones.
[38:29]

Discussion Question

1. Why is the method of critical thinking on the verses of the Quran emphasized so much in the Quran itself?

Satan's Judgment of His Value

Satan said:
"I am better than Adam.
You created me from fire but him from lowly dirt."
[38:76]

Discussion Question

1. How did Satan judge the value of a creation?

Satan's Request to God

Satan said:
"Oh my Merciful Safeguarding God!
Please allow me till the Last Day on the earth
So that I can show You that I am right
God said:
"You are granted permission
Till to a known Day"
[38:79–81]

Commentary

According to the verse above, everything happens with the permission of God but there is a wisdom and reason behind.

Discussion Question

1. Why was Satan so determined in asserting his perceived superiority over Adam?

39. Opening the Chest and Heart

The Chest

A fa man sharaha Allahu sadrahu lil Islami fa huwa ala nurin min Rabbih

When God opens the person's chest, soul and heart for the true guidance, and submission and then, this person becomes now on the peaceful, delightful path of joy and happiness from her or his Loving and Nourishing God

Fa waylun lil qasiyati qulubuhum min dhikrllah
After this,
How unfortunate are the ones whose hearts become hardened due to not remembering God?

Ulaika fi dalalin Mubin
These ones are on a clear misguidance.
[39:22]

Commentary

The above verse is presented with its transliteration. The transliterated text from Arabic is presented to convey the original poetic sounds. In practice, some people, especially Sufis, often read this verse in the mornings to open their "spiritual hearts." In fact, they assert that if the verse is read early in the morning before breakfast and before conversing with others, this spiritual immersion is more effective.

Discussion Questions

1. What are the effects of sounds on the human heart and mind?
2. Without knowing its meaning, how do you perceive the word "sharaha"? How does the word's transliterated pronunciation correspond with its meaning?
3. Why is it suggested to read certain phrases in the original language of revelation?

True Appreciation of the Divine

They were not showing the true Appreciation for God
The whole earth will be of a single grip with the Exalted Most High
    Merciful God on the Day of Judgment, and
The heavens will be rolled up like a paper with the order of the Creator.
Pure is God,
Far too high than what they falsely associate with
The Unique One God.
[39:67]

Commentary

The above verse can indicate awe and appreciation towards the Creator. In the Quran, there are verses that praise Christians, Jews, and any other people of faith that strive through prayers, chants, and inner reflections to establish and maintain a relationship with the Creator, and thus, appreciate God.

Discussion Question

1. How can one appreciate and be thankful to God in Islam?

40. Proving superiority through arguments?

For sure and clearly,
The ones who argue about Our verses and signs
Without any proof, logic, and reference

They do it only to show their superiority, and how great they are!
Don't worry,
They won't be able to reach the level of superiority that they desire.

After all this,
Seek refuge in God from their evil and harm.

Certainly,
God is Full Aware, Hearing and Seeing.
[40:56]

Discussion Questions

1. From the above verse, how can one understand the arguments about religion?
2. According to the above verse, what is authentic? What is the true knowledge and information about God?

41. Straight Path and Consistency

Straight Path and Consistency

For sure, the ones who say
"Our Merciful and All Caring Creator is God"
Then,
They continue on the straight path and middle way, and,
The angels descend on them and say:
"Don't worry, and don't be scared"
"Be happy with the heaven that is promised for you"
"We are your friends in this world and afterlife"
"You will get what you desire…."
"You will get what you want…."
"This is from the One who is the Most Forgiving, and the Most Merciful."
After all this,
Who has the best word and approach
Other than the ones:
Praying and appreciating God,
Doing always good
And saying
"I am from the Muslims, the ones who turned myself fully to God and accepted everything from my Only True Merciful Creator."
[41:30–33]

Discussion Questions

1. How can angels become friends with a person on the right path?
2. Why do angels console a person on the path?

Humility

Among God's signs are the night and the day, and the sun and the moon.
Do not prostrate yourselves to the sun, or to the moon, or anything else.

But prostrate yourselves to God who has created them,
If you only, and sincerely worship your One Creator.
Still, if they continue to show arrogance,
Then, those who are in the Loving, Merciful and Exalted Divine Presence
Worship to God, day and night, and
They do not get tired but take pleasure, sweetness and taste from it.
[41:37–38]

Discussion Question

1. How can one show humbleness and humility for God in prayers?

Language of the Scripture

And if we made this Quran in another language other than Arabic
Then, they for sure would have said
Shouldn't its verses be understood and explained?"
So, it will be a non-Arabic Book to an Arab messenger?
Does it make sense?

After this,
Tell them:
This Quran is a guidance and
A source of health for the ones who attained faith.
But as for those who won't believe
In their ears is deafness and
This book will be invisible and obscure to them.
As if they are being called from a very far distance.
[41:44]

Discussion Question

1. How does the above verse rationalize the language of the Quran?

42. How God Communicates with Humans

How God Communicates with Humans

And,
It is not possible for any mortal human that God speaks to this person
Except
By revelation

Or

From behind a veil with a means of a vehicle

Or

By sending a messenger (i.e., angel) with a revelation

Communicating the Divine messages with the permission of God.

After all, certainly,
God is Exalted, far from human thoughts and imaginations,
God is the source of Wisdom and Authority.
[42:51]

Discussion Questions

1. In Islam, according to the above verse, how can one understand God's communication with humans? Why?
2. Will there be a change in how God communicates with a person after death? If yes, how?

43. Angels and Speculations

Angels and Speculations

And,
They made false claims about angels:
By asserting that they are females.
They are only the creation and worshippers of God, the Most Merciful.
When they claim this,
Did they witness the creation of angels?

What a false claim!

They will soon be questioned
About their assertions.
[43:19]

Commentary

In Islam, it is important to believe in unseen without any speculations. A person can know about the unseen from the information which God provides in the scriptures. The first and foremost unseen is God. A Muslim should follow the guidelines in the scripture about who God is. In repeated verses of the Quran, the following statement is ordered by God to the Prophet Muhammad to convey the message of Who God is: "Tell them that I have been revealed that your Creator is One." Or in the chapter of unity [112], "Tell them that God is One and Unique. God was not born and does not give birth." Similarly, the life after death, angels, future, and destiny are some of these unseen as well. The above verse explains that people make speculations about angels by putting a gender on them and there is no information revealed about this claim of some humans. The verse refutes their claim.

Discussion Question

1. How can one increase his or her knowledge about the unseen with a genuine or authentic methodology in Islam?

44. Signs before the Earth's Termination

Signs before the Earth's Termination

After this,
Wait and expect for the day
When the sky is covered with an obvious smoke.
[44:10]

Commentary

According to expected prophecy by the Prophet[11], one of the signs before the full annihilation of the earth[83] is the sky being covered with smoke. The verse above mentions this prophecy.

Discussion Question

1. According to the Quran and Hadith, what are the other signs preceding a total annihilation of the earth?

---

83. Which is referred to as "end of time."

45. Accountability

Accountability

And that day
You will see
All the groups, people, communities
Humbling themselves before God by kneeling down,
All the groups, people, communities
Are being called to its record of accountability.

Today,
You will be rewarded or accountable about
What you have been doing on the earth in your life.
[45:28]

Commentary

The above verse explains the group as well as individual accountability. It is very important in Islam to side with the groups of ethical behavior and action although people may have different beliefs. However, as mentioned in Chapter 3, the Quran additionally calls Christians, Jews, and Muslims to the recognition and acceptance of their common One Creator and accordingly work together for the good not falsehood.

Discussion Question

1. In Islam, what is the difference between group and individual accountability before God?

46. The Mother, the Father, and the Child

The Mother, the Father, and the Child

We required the person
To be nice, grateful and kind to their parents

This person's mother had a pregnancy and delivery,
With difficulty and pain,

And, even with difficulty
Pregnancy and Breast feeding
Can take up to thirty months.
[46:15]

Commentary

According to some commentators of the Quran, the soul descends unto a baby's body three months after conception and thus, the fetus in a mother's womb is only recognized as an individual human being after the first trimester of pregnancy. Most scholars interpret the 30 months indicated in the verse to include both the second and third trimesters (6 months in sub-total), and the recommended period (24 months) of breastfeeding as encouraged in Islam.

Discussion Questions

1. In Islam, what are the rights of a parent with respect to a child?
2. How can one understand the Quran's specific numbers about pregnancy, child formation in the womb, and breastfeeding? How can one compare it with current scientific data in gynecology?

47. Know That There Is No Deity except God

Know That There Is No Deity except Allah

After all this,

Know certainly without any doubt!
That
There is no deity, god, except God, Allah.

And, therefore,

Constantly be in the state of asking forgiveness
For your forgetfulness, heedlessness and carelessness in your relationship
With your true, only, very Merciful and Caring and One God

And, also ask forgiveness
For your fellow brothers and sisters as well.

God knows your change
From one place to another
From one spiritual state to another
From one struggle to another

And,

God also knows your place of station
Where you will end in this world.
Where you will end in the afterlife.
[47:19]

Discussion Questions

1. Why is the full belief in One God the core of Islam? How does the above verse represent this creed?
2. How can one understand transitions in faith *(change)* and final situation *(station)* as described in the above verse?

48. Tranquility and Calmness on the Heart

Tranquility and Calmness on the Heart

God is the One who
Poured tranquility[84] and calmness into the hearts of the believers

So that,

Their existing belief and trust in God can increase
With more and more trust and belief.

And Remember!
All the forces of the skies and earth belong to God

And Remember!
God is always All Knowing, All Source of Wisdom and Authority.
[48:4]

Discussion Question

1. In Islam, what is the understanding of tranquility (Sakina) in the heart? How can this tranquility permeate and establish itself in the heart of a person?

---

84. Sakina in Ar.

49. Social and Ethnic Classifications

Social and Ethnic Classifications

Oh people!
Indeed,
We have created you as males and females.

And after that,
We put you in different nations, social, ethnic and kinship groups

So that,
You have the interest and motivation to know each other.

But Remember!
Certainly and for sure,
The best and highest of you among all of these groups
Is the one who has appreciation, and consciousness of God

Indeed, Remember!
God is All Knowing, All Aware of your Engagements.
[49:13]

Commentary

Only the Creator is aware of a genuine God consciousness. Therefore, apart from God, no one has the authority in a real sense to judge or value any other person. If adopted in societies, this principle can help to eliminate any type of discrimination in our modern social life.

Discussion Question

1. According to Islam, what is the purpose of the different ethnic, national, racial, and social classifications?

50. Escape from Death

Closer than Jugular Veins

Certainly,
We created the person and
We know what type of temptations one's own self constantly whispers and
We are closer to this person than this person's own jugular veins
[50:16]

Discussion Question

1. What does it mean to be closer to someone than his/her own *"jugular"* veins?

The Intoxication of Death

The intoxication of death[85] has now come for sure,
That was the part you always tried to escape.
[50:19]

Discussion Question

1. What does the intoxication of death mean in theology?

---

85. Sakratul Mawt in Ar.

51. Escape to God

Escape to God

After all this,
"Escape to God!
Run to God!"

Certainly and for sure,
I am an obvious and straightforward
Warning Messenger
To you from God
[51:50]

Commentary

As in the previous chapter (Chapter 50), the same word for escape (*"firar"* in Arabic language) is used in this chapter. Connecting the contextual meanings in the two consecutive chapters encourages a return to God via death. In particular, the word, *"firar"* in Sufi terminology has a lot of embedded meaning that suggests fostering a spiritual connection with the Creator.

Discussion Question

1. What does "escaping or running" to God mean in the above verse?

Benefit of Advice

After all this, give them advice!
For sure,
Advice will benefit at least some, who have attained faith in God.
And remember!
"I created the Jinn[86] and humans only to
Recognize, appreciate, and worship Me."
[51:55–56]

Discussion Question

1. What is the etiquette of giving advice in Islam?

---

86. Jinn are other creations of God other than humans. They are also accountable for their actions and choices in life. They are unseen creatures from a unique creation often thought of as ghost like creatures.

52. God as the Just and the Merciful in Accountability

And that Day, after the completion of questioning and accountability,

They will be dragged to imprisonment and punishment.

The officers will say:

"Isn't this the punishment that you were denying its existence in your life on the earth?

Look now! Is this punishment magic or illusion? Don't you see now?

You will be imprisoned and punished and doesn't matter if you are patient or not.

As a justice, you are all being paid back now for your ungratefulness to God, your evil and oppression to other humans and all other creations that you have been constantly preoccupied with in the world."

On the contrary,

Certainly and for sure,
The ones who are respectful of God and being ethical, just and fair to humans
Will be in gardens and pleasure
Enjoying what their Generous and Merciful has given them, and
Their Caring and Appreciative God protected them from the punishment and imprisonment.

The friendly officers will say:
"Indulge in all pleasures, eating, drinking....
With the mercy of God,
You are all being paid back now
For your regular respect and worship of God,

For being ethical, just and fair to humans and all other creations,
Which you were persistently being preoccupied with in the world."
[52:13-19]

Discussion Question

1. According to the above verse and others, how can we understand these attributes of God: "The Just" and "The Merciful"?

53. Following a Fantasy

The Star

With the name of God, the All-Merciful, the Very-Merciful.
By the star, when it goes down to set,
[53:1]

Commentary

There are several referrals to night journeys in the divine scriptures. In the Quran, several chapters are named after the Night and its elements: Star, Moon, etc. A chapter is also named after the Sun. As described in the Quran, the physical and spiritual journeys of Moses and Muhammad occurred during the night. Moses' encounter with the burning bush was in the night. Similarly, Prophet Muhammad's ascension to the heavens is believed to occur in the night.

Discussion Question

1. According to the Quran, what is the significance of the stars?

Following a Fantasy

For sure,
These are the names
That you and your forefathers made up about God.
God did not send any proof about it.
They just follow an ungrounded fantasy.
They just follow what their egos' desire
About knowing God.

However, think and look!
Certainly,
The Guidance, the Quran, came to them from their Merciful God.
[53:23]

Discussion Question

1. Is it common for people to call God according to their own deductions? According to the above verse and others, what makes those deductions about God true or whimsical?

54. The Easy Quran

The Easy Quran

And,
For Sure and Definitely,
We made the Quran easy in mind
As a Book of Remembrance
As a Book of Chant
As a Book of Worship
As a Book of Advice

After all this,
Is there anyone who will take it to the heart?
Is there anyone who will take advice from it?
Is there anyone of who will take it as a book of chant and worship?
[54:17, 22, 32, 40]

Commentary

The above verse is repeated four times in this chapter.

Discussion Questions

1. According to the exegetical scholars, what is the purpose of repetition in the Quran?
2. What are the different names of the Quran? Why?

55. Which favors of your Merciful, Nourishing, and Caring God will you deny?

Which favors of your Merciful, Nourishing, and Caring God will you deny?

After all this,

Which favors of your Merciful, Nourishing, and Caring God will you deny?

[55:13, 16, 18, 21, 23, 25, 28, 30, 32, 34, 36, 38, 40, 42, 45, 47, 49, 51, 53, 55, 57, 59, 61, 63, 65, 67, 69, 71, 73, 75, 77]

Commentary

The above verse is repeated thirty-one times in the above chapter and it is addressed to men, women, and the Jinn.[87] In style, this chapter is different from other chapters in the Quran. The verse is repeated after a bounty bestowed by God is identified in the chapter.

Discussion Questions

1. What is the importance of this chapter in practice?
2. How can one compare the style of this chapter with other chapters in the Quran?

Not Worshiping God Due to Preoccupation

Ar-Rahman,

The Most Merciful and the Most Caring,

Taught you the Quran.

Created the person.

Taught this person how to speak and express him or herself.

Remember!

The sun and the moon are on a specific orbit with precise calculation.

[55:1–5]

---

87. The Jinn are the unseen creation of God similar to humans. The Jinn also have their own life span, the free will, and accountability of their actions in front of God.

Discussion Questions

1. As the chapter starts with one of the names of God, the Most Merciful and the Most Caring, Ar-Rahman, what can be the reason for this type of beginning for this chapter?
2. How can one interpret the understanding of the precise calculation of the sun and moon in the above verse?

56. Coordinates of Stars in the Universe

Drinking Pure Wine

They will drink bowls and jugs and a goblet of pure wine,
From which they will neither suffer headache,
Nor will they be intoxicated.
[56:18–19]

Commentary

In the above description, one of the drinks in Heaven will be wine. It will only give pleasure. There will not be any side effects from it. There will not be any pain of headache, migraine, or vomiting unlike other alcoholic drinks in this world. The worldly pleasures can have side effects but the pleasures in Heaven will be without it. According to the Muslim mystics, Sufis, a person drinks a better spiritual wine in life compared to the normal wine if one gets intoxicated with the spiritual ecstasy of the Divine.

Discussion Questions

1. What is the difference between physical and spiritual intoxication?
2. Compared to wine consumption, how can one experience more pleasure by being spiritually intoxicated?

Coordinates of Stars in the Universe

After this,
I swear and affirm on the precise location, coordinates of each star in the universe.
And Certainly and Absolutely,
This affirmation is an enormous and critical statement if you scientifically know.
Certainly and definitely,
This is the Noble Quran,
This Quran is well-protected and guarded, original and pure.

Therefore,
The impure should not touch it.
[56:75–79]

Commentary

In the above verses, God is underlining the importance of coordinates of each star in the galaxies in the balance of all the systems of the universe. Muslims cannot touch the original revelation of the Quran in Arabic unless they physically perform a washing ritual called wudhu or ghusl. The verse "the impure should not touch it" indicates this ruling in Islam.

Discussion Question

1. What is the importance and interpretation of coordinates of each star in present astronomy? How can one interpret this information with the above verse?

57. Hardened Hearts and Remembrance of God

Hardened Hearts and Remembrance of God

Has the time not come for the believers and appreciators of God
That their hearts be humble and tremble at the remembrance of God
And even all the truth is revealed to them?

After this,
Do not be like those who are given the Divine revelations before
And still their hearts become hardened after a long time passed
And most of them are lost-wanderers.[88]
[57:16]

Commentary

The above verse is mentioned in the Chapter of Iron (Chapter Number 57). In modern chemistry, one of the isotopes of iron in the periodic table is Iron-57, a stable isotope widely used in Spectroscopy. According to the modern commentators, this observation is not an ordinary coincidence and it is regarded as one of the many miracles of the Quran. Also, it is interesting to note that the verse is mentioned in the Chapter of Iron where God attributes hardening of the heart to the failure of remembering the Creator. In practice, if a person fails to establish regular rituals, prayers, chantings, or other practices in the remembrance of God, then the person's heart becomes hardened and it will be susceptible and vulnerable to different spiritual diseases.

Discussion Questions

1. How does one's heart become hardened physically and spiritually?
2. How does remembrance of God soften one's heart in practice?

---

88. Fasiq is translated as lost wanderer due to the context of the verse.

58. Secret Conversations

Secret Conversations

Have you not observed that God knows everything in the skies, in
 space, in the galaxies and everything in the earth?
No secret conversation takes place between three, but God is the fourth
 of them,
Nor between five, but God is the sixth of them,
Neither between fewer than that nor more,
But God is with them wherever they are.
Then at the end,
God will tell them on the Day of Judgment what they did.
Surely, God is All-Knowing and All Aware about everything.
[58:7]

Discussion Question

1. What is the ethical teaching of the above verse in Islam?

59. Self and God

Self and God

Oh you who believe in God!
Have respect, and appreciation for God!

Every person should consider
What they prepare for tomorrow
What they prepare for tomorrow
For the Day of Judgement

Have respect and appreciation of God!
    God is aware of what you are constantly engaged in.

Don't be like the ones that forget God
Then, God made them forget their own selves

These are the lost wanderers.[89]
[59:18–19]

Discussion Question

1. If a person forgets himself/herself, does he/she forgets God as well?

---

89. Fasiq is translated as lost wanderer due to the context of the verse.

60. Enemies Becoming Friends

Enemies Becoming Friends

It is possible that
God can make friendship
Between you and your enemies
God is All Powerful to do anything.

After this, Remember!
Indeed,
God is All Forgiving about the past if you sincerely regret, repent and ask forgiveness
Because
God is All Merciful and Caring about the creation.
[60:7]

Discussion Questions

1. What is the message of the above verse?
2. How do the Muslims incorporate the teaching of this verse in their lives?
3. According to a hadith narration, what is the story of the serial killer who killed one hundred people?

61. Advising What You Don't Practice

Advising What You Don't Practice

Oh you who attained faith in God
Why do you say things and advise people
That you don't do and practice yourself.

Most loathsome in the sight of God are the ones
Who advise people
But they don't do themselves
[61:2–3]

Discussion Question

1. What should be the ethics of counseling others according to the above verse?

62. Run Away from Death

Say,
For sure,
the death that you are trying to run away from
Definitely will visit you as well.
After,
You will be returned to
the One, Knower of all Unseen and Unknowns,
the One, Knower of all Seen and Knowns.
So that,
The One, God will inform about the true reality of your engagements
    in the world.
[62:8]

Discussion Question

1. Why does the person want to escape from death?

63. Not Worshipping God Due to Being Busy

Not Worshipping God Due to Being Busy

Oh You who attained faith and trust in God!
Make sure your preoccupation
With your work
With your family
Do not stop you remembering, and worshipping your
All Merciful and All Caring Creator
Whoever stops appreciating and remembering God
For sure,
This person becomes only a loser in this world and afterlife.
[63:9]

Discussion Questions

1. Is it common for people to stop their religious duties due to their preoccupations with work and family?
2. What is the major teaching in the above verse?

64. As Much as You Can

As Much as You Can

After all this,
Have fear, love and respect of God
As much as you can!

Pay attention!
Follow the teachings of God,
Help the poor and needy
All above are good and beneficial for you.

After all this,
Whoever protects oneself
From his or her own caprice, misery, and evil

Then,
It is those who will be
Happy and successful.
In this life and after death.
[64:16]

Discussion Questions

1. According to Islamic theology, what does "have fear, respect and love of God as much as you can" from the above verse mean in practice?
2. What is the caprice and evil of one toward one's own self in the above verse?

65. Financial Concerns in Divorce

Financial Concerns in Divorce

And remember!
For all the financial concerns in divorce,
God can provide livelihood, sustenance and money
From a source that this person does not expect at all,

After all this,
Whoever truly relies and trusts in God
God is sufficient for that person.
For sure,
God's decision is always and perfectly fulfilled.

And remember!
For sure and definitely,
God makes balance in everything.
[65:3]

Commentary

The above lines are from the verse that contextually mentions the difficulties of divorce and its financial concerns and conflicts between the spouses before, during, and after the process. It is important to remember that God can provide livelihood and sustenance for the person who may be much concerned about the financial burden of divorce during its process and after it.

Discussion Question

1. Is it common for people to keep or break their marriages due to financial fears?

66. Two Model Women: Virgin Mary and the Wife of Pharaoh

The Wife of Pharaoh

And Remember,
God brings a model for the believers
The example of the wife of the pharaoh

When she said secretly:
"Oh God, prepare a royal residence for me in Heaven and
Save me from pharaoh and his oppression and
Save me from the group of oppressors."
[66:11]

Commentary

One of the role models (women) in Islam is the wife of Pharaoh. She was not in support of her husband's oppression towards the children of Israel. Secretly, she made prayers to God to seek forgiveness and protection from Pharaoh's oppression in this world and the hereafter. A cardinal principle in Theology is not to support oppressors and tyrants. According to the Prophet, there exists three levels of condemning and/or changing evil: The first level is stopping and confronting evil(s) by all means, the second level is a verbal condemnation of the evil, and the third (lowest) level is to detest the evil action even though you are incapable of doing anything about it.[11]

Discussion Question

1. Why is the position of wife of pharaoh special in Islam?

Virgin Mary

And Remember,
God brings a model for the believers
The example of Virgin Mary, the daughter of Joachim.

Virgin Mary is the one
Who protected her chastity and piety
And accordingly,
From Our pool of the souls,
We breathed a soul into Jesus.
Then,
Virgin Mary
Testified and witnessed to the truth of the words of her
Merciful Creator and the Divine books,
She was one of the pious and devout in appreciating the favors of God.
[66:12]

Discussion Question

1. According to the above verse and others in Islamic theology, what is special about the birth of baby Jesus?

67. Birds

Birds

Don't they see the birds above them,
Flying in groups, spreading and folding their wings,
With involuntary and voluntary drives,
None but the Most Merciful and Gracious One holds them in the air
Definitely, God is aware and watchful of everything
[67:19]

Discussion Question

1. How do Muslims interpret scientific explanations about natural events?

68. Grasping with the Eyes

The ones who are bent on denying the truth would almost grasp and
 kill you with their eyes whenever they hear this reminder…
[68:51]

Commentary

The above line alludes to the negative effect of the "evil eye" on humans. Islam accepts the existence of the "evil eye" and suggests some ways to be protected from it. To protect themselves from evil and attract good fortune, some Muslims print the above expressions from the Quran and place them in different parts of the homes, offices, or vehicles. Alternatively, with the Prophet's suggestions, they read some daily litanies or prayers of protection.

Discussion Question

1. What does "grasp with their eyes" from the above verse mean?

69. Very Little Thinking, Reflection, and Belief

Very Little

For sure and definitely,

This book is the word of a
Noble Messenger and
Not the word of a poet but
Very little you believe

And this book is
Not the word of a magician but
Very little you think and reflect

Revealed in pieces from the
the Merciful and Caring Creator of all the universe, heavens and galaxies.
[69:40–43]

Discussion Question

1. According to exegetical interpretations of the Quran, what does the phrase "very little" in the above verse signify in critical thinking?

And for Sure

And for sure,
this Book is a Reminder
For the ones
who have respect, humbleness, and fairness

And for sure,
Definitely, We know that
Some of you will not accept and will deny

And for sure,
This Book is disappointing for the deniers

And for sure,
This Book is certainly the absolute Truth

After all this,
Don't worry about them!
Move on!
Turn to your Merciful God!
Glorify and Connect to
Your Creator
With the Most Exalted and Highest Name
[69:48–52]

Discussion Questions

1. In the above verse, how can one interpret the notion of "certainty"? Why?
2. How can a person use the scripture for his/her benefit and for others?

70. Elevators and Paths

Elevators and Paths

From God,
There are countless elevators and paths
In order to spiritually climb up.
[70:3]

Commentary

The above translation is similar to Muhammad Asad's[13] rendering. The verse encourages everyone to establish a relationship with God. There exists various spiritual paths in establishing a relationship with the Divine.

Discussion Question

1. What is meant by "elevators and paths" in the above verse?

71. My House

My House

Oh my Merciful, Safeguarding, and Caring God!
Forgive me,
Forgive my parents
Forgive everyone who enters my house as a person of appreciation and believer of You
Forgive all the men and women who appreciates and attains faith in You

And as for the oppressors, the evil doers and evil planners
Counter their evil and oppression with a satisfactory and better encounter
[71:28]

Commentary

Above is a prayer of Prophet Noah mentioned in the Quran. He asks forgiveness from God for everyone. As the Prophet Noah and his followers were weak in the society they were not able to counter the oppression against the oppressors except asking and praying to God for protection against their evil. In Arabic, there are different words for house such as al-bayt which is used in this verse. Another word for house is maskan which means the place of tranquility, calmness, and sakina.

Discussion Questions

1. What is the place of a house in Islam?
2. How can the above prayer of seeking God's blessings for visitors and guests be interpreted?

72. The unseen beings and the humans, dare to lie against God?

The unseen beings and the humans, dare to lie against God?

The unseen beings, Jinns said:
"And,
Certainly,
Our Merciful God is Exalted, the Most High
Does not have any children
Does not have any equivalent or spouse.
And,
But still the ignorant ones among us
Are saying nonsense things about God.

And,
Indeed,
We thought that
The humans and the Jinn, unseen beings[90]
Will not dare to lie against God."
[72:3–5]

Discussion Questions

1. What are the unseen beings?
2. "We" in the verse refers to?
3. What do the unseen beings find ridiculous about the false claims (made by the ignorant ones) against God?

---

90. Jinn is translated as unseen beings similar to rendering of M. Asad [13]. Like humans, Jinn have their own life, death, and accountability in front of God.

73. Importance of Nights Compared to Daytime

Importance of Nights Compared to Daytime

The time spent at *Night*
in worship,
in chant and
in prayers to God
is
More strong and satisfactory
For heart and tongue
Compared to the *Daytime*
Because, for sure,
You get busy in the day time.
[73:6–7]

Commentary

Several sayings of Prophet Muhammad and verses of the Quran encourage night prayers and worship.

Discussion Question

1. In Islam, why are the night prayers more valuable in comparison to daytime prayers?

74. Clean Dress, Clean Body, and Clean Heart

Clean Dress, Clean Body, and Clean Heart

Oh who is secluded, folded and cloaked
Get up and inform people about God
Glorify the Greatness of your Merciful and Nourishing Creator
Always keep your dress and heart clean
Always keep your body and heart away from filth and evil

After this,
Do not compromise from your principles to acquire more
But
Continue to be patient
In the path of your Merciful and Caring God.
[74:1–7]

Discussion Question

1. How is external cleanliness related to internal cleanliness in Islam? How is this principle applied in five daily prayers for Muslims?

75. Fingerprints

Fingerprints

I swear by the Day of Resurrection
And I swear by the self-blaming self
Does man think that We cannot assemble his or her bones?
Yes, certainly We can do it.
Even, We can resurrect the humans from their fingerprints.
[75:1–4]

Commentary

Modern interpreters use these verses to assert the miraculous nature of the Quran. Without access to advanced technology or modern forensic knowledge, the Quran (revealed about 1,400 years ago) clearly confirms the uniqueness of an individual's fingerprints. In our modern world, fingerprint technology is now widely used for accurate identification and forensic investigations.

Discussion Question

1. With the insight of scientific and technologies discoveries, how do the modern commentators explain and interpret the Quran?

Self-Awareness

For sure,
The person is aware of their own self
But at the same time making up excuses
[75:14–15]

Discussion Question

1. Does "self-awareness" in the verses reference this worldly life or the life after death?

76. The Human Being

The Human Being

Don't you know
Billions of years passed
Human being was not
Worthy of mention

Then, We created the human
From a microscopic size embryo
Then, testing this person
While this person seeing and hearing

We gave this person a free choice
A choice of recognition and appreciation
Or a choice of unrecognition and unappreciation
[76:1–3]

Discussion Questions

1. What is the original word for "billions of years" in the scripture? Does this word have any significance in the literature?
2. In this translation, to whom does recognition and appreciation refer to?

77. Embarrassment, Humiliation, and Denying the Truth

Embarrassment, Humiliation, and Denying the Truth

Didn't We create you from a simple water, a fluid of sperm?
Then, We put this with the egg in a firm place, to the womb.
Till to a known time of pregnancy and delivery

After all,
We determined everything!
How excellent everything We arranged and determined!

After all this,
If they don't recognize and appreciate God
How embarrassing and humiliated are those
On that Day
Who deny these truths
[77:20–24]

Commentary

The expression "how embarrassing are those on that Day who deny these truths" is repeated ten times in this chapter.

Discussion Question

1. What could be reasons for repeating the above expression in this chapter?

Which word after this Quran?

When they are told to
Appreciate and Respect to God
By worship and bowing

If they still don't do it
How embarrassing and humiliated are those
On that Day
Who deny these truths

After all this,
If they don't believe in this Quran
Which other word will they believe in?
[77:48–50]

Discussion Question

1. What is the position of the Quran compared to other words in Islamic theology?

78. The Great Event

The Great Event

Do you know about what they are asking each other all the time?
About the Great Event!
About which they speculate and dispute
Don't Worry!
Certainly, they will know soon about it
Don't Worry!
For sure,
They will know soon about it.
[78:1–5]

For Sure,
This Day, the Great Event
Is True and Real.
After all this,
Whoever wants
Can prepare an acceptable path
To their Merciful, Forgiving and Caring Creator
[78:39]

Commentary

The "Great Event" is another name of the Day of resurrection and accountability.

Discussion Question

1. What is the teaching of the Prophet about the Last Day of the earth and the Day of resurrection?

79. Extractors

(Soul) Extractors

With the name of Allah, the All-Merciful, the Very-Merciful.
I swear by those who extract with great force
I swear by those who extract smoothly
I swear by those who float and swim swiftly,
Then, those who compete with each other
Then, those who arrange the matters
On the Day, when the shocking event will shock everything
[79:1–6]

Discussion Question

1. What is the context of the actions in the above verses?

80. Preference in Teaching

Frowned and turned away
When the blind came
How do you know
Maybe the blind will benefit from the spiritual purification
When reminded about God
Maybe even this reminder will have a benefit

But,
The one who is arrogant and does not care
You give attention to this person

While no blame is expected of you
If this arrogant person does not attain any purity.
[80:1–7]

Discussion Question

1. According to the above verse, who should be given preference to teach when someone wants to learn?

81. Wrapping up the Sun

Wrapping up the Sun

With the name of Allah, the All-Merciful, the Very-Merciful.
When the sun is wrapped up and
When the stars are fallen down and
When the mountains are set in motion,
When all the valuables[91] are abandoned and
When all the wild animals are gathered and
When the seas are lit up with fire and
When all the humans are paired with their engagements and
When the murdered female children will be resurrected and
    questioned
about their murderer and for what sin she was killed for and
When the scrolls (of deeds) will be unscrolled and
When the sky will be ripped off and
When the punishments are prepared and
When Heaven and rewards are brought close

NOW
The soul knows what it has brought
and which direction it is going
[81:1–14]

Discussion Question

1. Compared to other texts. how can we interpret the content and style of the above verses?

---

91. I'saru in all the translations are as pregnant camel. It has the contextual meaning of being a very valuable asset for the Arabs. Therefore, contextual meaning was preferred for the contemporary time.

82. Deception

Deception

Oh man!
What is constantly deceiving you about your Gracious, Loving, and
    Merciful God,
Who created you,
Then perfected you,
Then made you in balance and proportion
In a form, color, face, and body according to the Divine choice

After all this,
Are you still denying the religion, the Day of Judgment and
    Accountability?
No!
(For sure, you are making a huge mistake!
And,
Still tempting to tell a lie and use an excuse)
[82:6–9]

Discussion Questions

1. How do the above verses establish connection between the creation of the human beings and the need of a religion and accountability after death?
2. What is the significance of this chapter?
3. What are the different themes covered in this chapter?

83. Cheating

Shame on those!
Who cheat and deceive people
But when they receive their due from people
They demand in full
But, when their due is to give,
They give less than it's due

Do they not know that they will be raised from the dead? and
Called for accountability on an Overpowering Nerve Wrecking Day!
The Day,
When all men shall stand before the Sustainer and Creator of all the
    worlds and universes!
[83:1–6]

Discussion Question

1. How can understanding and interpretation of above verses help the person live an ethical life?

84. Earth, Sky, and Their Relationship with God

Earth and Sky and Their Relationship with God

With the name of Allah, the All-Merciful, the Very-Merciful

When the sky cracks and splits and
Listens to the command of its Creator
As it should listen and

When the earth is stretched
And throws up and empties whatever it contains, and
Listens to the command of its Creator
As it should listen

(See now! what every person has brought forth for their struggle in life)

Oh man!
You are in constant engagement and struggle
Until you meet with your Merciful and Just God
Finally, and Certainly,
You will meet with your Creator
[84:1–6]

Discussion Question

1. How does the above verse portray the position of the sky and the earth in their relationship with God?

85. Love of God

Love of God

For sure, the grasp of your Merciful Safeguarding God is so strong
For sure, God is the One who creates, re-creates and resurrects
And for sure, God is the Most-Forgiving, the Most-Loving,
And for sure, God is the Owner of the Exalted Authority, Control and
 Dominion
[85:12–15]

Discussion Question

1. How is the love of God understood in Islam compared to Christianity, Judaism, and other religions?

86. Human Embryo Fertilization and Implantation

Human Fertilization and Implantation

Does the person look what he or she was created from?
Created from a discharged fluid of sperm and an egg
Coming from between the loins and the pelvic arch
Of a man and a woman
For a human fertilization and implantation

After all this,
Certainly, definitely, and for sure,
Allah has the power to recreate after death
For a Day,
Where all the secrets are exposed
And the person does not have
Neither strength nor supporter or helper

Here is another example:

For sure, when the sky sends the rain like sperm
For sure, when the earth cracks open like an egg
For a fertilization and implantation

After all this,
Certainly, for sure and definitely,
This Quran is a separator between the truth and falsehood

I swear
This is not a joke!
[86:5–14]

Discussion Questions

1. Why is there so much emphasis on resurrection and accountability after death in the Quran?
2. With the advent of increased scientific knowledge in reproduction and embryology, how do modern Quranic commentators explain the analogy of *"rain from the sky and cracking of the earth"* in the formation and development of the human embryo?

87. Success and Purification of the Heart

Success and Purification of the Heart

For sure, success is achieved
By purifying the heart

For sure, success is achieved
By chanting, glorifying and appreciating your Merciful, Caring and Generous God
For sure, success is achieved
By offering the daily prayers

But,
You prefer this worldly temporal life,
While
Afterlife is much better and permanent.

And even for sure,
This teaching was written in the previous scriptures
In the script of Abraham
And
In the script of Moses, the Torah
[87:14–19]

Discussion Questions

1. According to the above verses, how can success be attained by purifying the heart?
2. What is the method of purifying one's heart in the above verses?

88. Reminder

So,
Remind them,
You are only a reminder
You are not over them a compeller or a controller.

After this,
Who turns away and does not recognize the Creator
Will have the greatest accountability by the Creator

For Sure, to Us is their return.
Then,
For sure,
Upon Us is their account.
[88:21–26]

Discussion Questions

1. What is the role of messengers, prophets, or Muslims in the task of preaching and giving advice to others?
2. What is the ideal method of advice in Islam?

89. The Happy Self

The Satisfied and Happy Self

Oh satisfied, content and happy self!
Come back to your Merciful and Forgiving God,
You will be satisfied, content and happy; because
Your Appreciative and Forgiving God is pleased with you for your good effort in the world,

After this, God will invite them and say:
"Enter among My special worshippers and
Enter My Heaven."
[89:28-30]

Commentary

In the above portion of the chapter, the self or the soul is pleased and God is pleased. According to Muslims, the ultimate goal in this world is to perform all the spiritual struggles to please God. If God is pleased, the person will be happy, content, and peaceful in this world and in the afterlife. Attaining Heaven is not the fundamental goal—rather it is a reward for the spiritual struggles.

Humility, especially in the relationship with the Divine, is of paramount importance in the spiritual journeys of struggle. It is not humiliating for Muslims to humble themselves in the presence of their Creator. Rather, it is actually a desired state of elevation. Therefore, the word "A'bd" in this chapter, translated to English, has different meanings (such as worshiper, creation, servant, or slave). A literal translation of the word can occlude its contextual meaning. In one's relationship with God, being a worshiper, servant, or creation of the Divine is an honor. On the contrary, worshiping and being subservient to all other beings is a dishonor according to the understandings of Muslims.

Discussion Question

1. How can one reach the level of content self in life according to the teachings of Islam?

90. Two Eyes, Two Ears, and One Tongue

Two Eyes, Two Ears, and One Tongue

Does the person think that no one sees them?
Didn't We give this person
Two eyes

Didn't We give this person
One tongue

Didn't We give this person
Two ears

Didn't We show this person
Two ways:
The truth and the real
The false and the deception
[90:7–10]

Discussion Question

1. How should different arrangement of the body parts inspire the person according to the above verse?

91. Success and Failure of the Self

Success and Failure of the Self

By the sun and its emerging brightness and
By the moon when it reflects the sun
By the day when it displays with the sun and
By the night when it covers the sun and

By the sky and the One who built it, and
By the earth and the One who expanded it
By the self and the One who perfected it
Then, the One who
Gave the person the choice of
Evil and the immoral or the good and the piety

After all this,
Certainly and for Sure,
Success and happiness is in the
Physical and Spiritual Purification of the self
Failure and depression is in the
Pollution, sinful, and evil command of the self
[91:1–10]

Discussion Question

1. How can the success and failure of the self be attained according to the above verse?

Right of an Animal

The Prophet of God said to them:
"Be careful of the Creator's camel and let her drink from the water."

But they rejected the Prophet, (did not care about his advice) and
  killed her,
So their just God sent a severe punishment upon them
Because of their evil,
And applied justice
Without any fear of its consequence
[91:13–15]

Commentary

According to the above verse, there were some arrogant people who demanded a miracle from God. Miraculously, God sent them a camel and they accepted it as a miracle. One day, while this camel was drinking from a well, these conceited people killed the camel without justification, but to challenge God and their prophet. Due to this oppression, God dispensed justice by punishing these people.

Discussion Questions

1. What are the animal rights in Islam?
2. Do humans hesitate to administer justice based on its consequences?

92. The Night

The Night

When the night covers
When the day rises
When God creates males and females
For sure,
 At the end, your efforts are diverse

The ones who are generous and charitable
And have respect for God
And acknowledge and testify the beauty of all signs from God
Then, we make everything easy for them

The ones who always hold back
And have arrogance
And deny the beauty of all signs from God
Then, We make everything difficult for them
[92:1–10]

Discussion Questions

1. If one recognizes God, how can things become easy?
2. If one does not recognize God, how can things become difficult?

93. What Is after Will Be Better

What Is after Will Be Better[92]

In the morning hours,
In the night when it covers
Your Caring God did not leave you
and
Your Loving God does not hate you

What is after will be better
From before
Your Generous God will give you so much that
You will be pleased and satisfied

Didn't God find you orphaned
and give you shelter

Didn't God find you lost[93]
and guide you

Didn't God find you in hunger and in need
and provide for you

Therefore,
Do not oppress an orphan
And,
Do not turn down a person in need

Therefore, after all this,
Appreciate and Pronounce constantly
all the favors of Your Generous and Loving Creator
[93:1–11]

---

92. Inspired from M. Sells, "Selected passages of the Quran."[70]
93. Everyone is lost in reference to their prior times of not knowing and worshipping God in a true and genuine way. Therefore, the word "lost" is true for everyone at different levels. The word "lost" is not an accepted appropriate word if it is used for the Prophet Muhammad according to the traditional Islamic understanding. The Prophet was guided by God from his birth until his demise.

PART 2   Selected Passages from the Quran with Interpreted Meanings

Discussion Questions
1. What is the significance of the above chapter in a Muslim practice?
2. What is the teaching of the above verse in one's relationship with God when the person encounters the evil in life?

94. Open Chest

Open Chest

Didn't We open and expand your chest for you
So that you are in the state of peace and tranquility

And didn't We remove your burden,
Stress, and fear from you
Such a burden was
Cracking your back

After this,
Indeed, We increased your remembrance, and a good reputation of you

Remember!
Therefore,
For sure, with every hardship comes ease
For sure, with every hardship comes ease

Therefore,
When you have free time hold tight and don't waste it
But,
Indeed,
Turn fully to your only Merciful and Loving God with desire and
Establish a sweet relationship

Alam Nashrah Laka Sadraq
Wa wada'naa a'nka wizrak
Allazii anqada zahrak
Wa rafa'naa laka dhikrak
Fainna ma' al u'sri Yusra
Inna ma' al u'sri Yusra
Faiza faraghta fansab
Wai la Rabbika fargab
[94:1-8]

Commentary

There are certain chapters and verses in the Quran that could be recited for both ritualistic and spiritual fortification in everyday practice. This chapter in its original Arabic language is often recited against depression, physical (and spiritual) heart problems, anxiety, and sadness by some Muslims. According to some Islamic practices, the chapter may be recited continuously until the reader's heart finds solace and his/her emotions calm down. The transliterated text from Arabic is also presented to convey the rhythmic sounds in the original Arabic language that complement its experiential meanings in practice.

Discussion Questions

1. Does life evolve around a cycle of ease and hardship? Is this a religious teaching?
2. Do people live a life full of difficulties? Do they live a life full of ease?
3. Do the people read this chapter to treat any type of physical sickness?

95. Perfection in Human's Creation

Perfection in Human's Creation

Certainly,
We created each human with the best composition of
Both physical and spiritual perfection
[95:4]

Commentary

According to the verse, the composition of a human body is perfect: upright, symmetrical, and balanced in form and nature. According to the Islamic Scholars, relocating any parts of the human body to any alternate position brings about imperfection in body functions and coordination. Similarly, the spiritual faculties of a human are perfect and humans decode everything in the creation intrinsically. It is the free will of a person to continue in this bodily and spiritual perfection by recognizing and appreciating the Creator and fulfilling the Divine orders accordingly. Likewise, using one's physical and spiritual faculties is the choice of the person when committing evil.

Discussion Question

1. According to the remaining parts of the chapter, how can one oscillate between perfection and imperfection?

96. Read, think, and learn!

Read, think, and learn!

With the name of your Nourishing and Caregiving God, who created everything
Created the person from an embryonic cell

After this,

Read, think and learn!
Your Caring God is the Most Generous and Gracious
The One who taught the abilities of learning and writing, the use of the pen
Taught the person what they did not know

After all this,
For sure,
This person becomes arrogant and self-deceitful
Thinking themselves free of need
Thinking themselves self-sufficient

Don't Worry!
Surely and Certainly
To your Just and Merciful Creator is the return.
[96:1–8]

Commentary

This chapter is the very first verse of the Quran revealed to the Prophet. Since these verses were the initial revelation in the Quran, the scholars emphasize the importance of learning, education, and critical thinking that God teaches to all humans in understanding the religion and its relationship with all sciences.

Discussion Questions

1. How is the historical revelation of these verses in the Quran?
2. According to the scholars, why is the quest for knowledge ("Read") the first command of God in the Quran?

97. The Night of Power

The Night of Power

Indeed,
We revealed the Quran in the night of power, and
Do you know what the night of the power is?
The night of power is better than one thousand months
In this night descends many angels and Gabriel on the earth
With the permission of their Merciful and Forgiving God
Everywhere and every instant
Is in peace this night
Continues till the beginning of dawn
[97:1–5]

Commentary

This night has a special value in Muslim practice. It is the one night in the entire year that God sends special blessings on the earth for all the creation. Based on the prophetic traditions, it is believed that this night should be sought during the last ten nights of Ramadan in each Muslim lunar calendar year.

Discussion Questions

1. Why is this night better than one thousand months?
2. According to the Muslim scholars, why is the specific date of this night unknown?

98. What is the correct and true religion for Christians and Jews?

What is the correct and true religion for Christians and Jews?

With the name of God, the All-Merciful, the Very-Merciful,
The People of the Book,
Christians, and Jews
Were not ordered except:
To worship only One God sincerely
As this has always been the correct religion of God[94]
Worshipping no one, but only One Creator

And, after this very first pillar
Establishing and Continuing to pray
Daily and regularly
And, at the same time
Sharing what were given to them: wealth, knowledge, and kindness

Certainly,
This has been always the correct and true religion.
[98:5]

Discussion Questions

1. How do you interpret the correct and true religion definition?
2. Why are the Christians and Jews especially addressed in the above verse?
3. According to the verses of the Quran, why do the Christians and Jews have double reward from God when they become Muslims compared to the Muslims who were born in Muslim families?

---

94. Rendering for "lahuddiin"

99. Atom's Weight of Good or Evil

Atom's Weight of Good or Evil

After death,
That Day,
People appear in groups
To be shown the reality of their actions

So that,
Who has an atom's weight of good
Will receive its reward

Who has an atom's weight of evil and oppression
Will face its accountability
[99:6–8]

Discussion Question

1. What is the accountability after death in Islam?

100. Self-Witnessing the Ungratefulness

Self-Witnessing the Ungratefulness

For sure,
The human being is unappreciative with their
Real Care Giver, God

And
But for sure,
This person knows their ungrateful behavior
As a fact and as a self-witness
[100:6–7]

Discussion Question

1. How can one witness his or her unappreciative behavior in one's relationship with God?

101. Mercy and Justice of God

After all,
For sure,
The ones whose scale is heavy of good deeds
Will be in the best life after death with the mercy of God
The ones whose scale is light of good deeds
Will be engulfed by an abyss with justice
Due to what this person deserves
[101:6–9]

Discussion Question

1. How does the justice and mercy of God work in this world and afterlife in Islam?

102. Knowing with Certainty

Boasting with your numbers: wealth, children, and degrees
Till you go down into your graves

Indeed, you will soon know the truth
Definitely, you will soon know the truth

Indeed, if you know the truth with knowledge
Then, you would understand the accountability, reward and punishment
Then, you will understand and realize everything with certainty
That, for sure, you will be questioned about everything at the end.
[102:1–8]

Discussion Questions

1. What are the levels of knowledge?
2. Do people boast with their acquisition of higher education (Bachelors, Masters, Doctorate, or MD degrees)? According to this chapter, do these accomplishments have any significance when the person dies?

103. Importance of Time

Importance of Time

Certainly,
The time passes but
The person is in loss
Except the ones
who are in submission and surrender to their one and only God and
who do always the good and ethical action and
who remind each other of reality and
who remind each other of patience.
[103:1–3]

Discussion Questions

1. What is your understanding of the message in this chapter?
2. Why is "and" (instead of "or") used to define the ones who are not in loss?
3. Why do people feel anxious as they age and get close to death? What is the significance of time?
4. When do people need patience? How do people remind each other about patience?

104. Slanderer and the Mean Person

Slanderer and the Mean Person

In the loss are every
Slanderer,
Fault-finder
Mocker,
Backbiter,
The mean person
The one relentlessly collects, stocks, and counts all his or her wealth
Thinking that this wealth will not last with the death
[104:1–3]

Discussion Question

1. According to the chapter, why are the slanderers, fault-finders, mockers, backbiters, and the mean people in a state of loss? What does "in loss" mean in the chapter?

105. Holy Sites and Invalidation of the Evil Plans by God

Did you see
How your Protector and Preserver, God, dealt with the people coming for destruction with the elephants?
Did you see
how God invalidated their evil plans?
[105:1–2]

Discussion Questions

1. What is the incident of elephants in the history of Kabah?
2. According to this chapter, how do Muslim scholars interpret the protection of the holy sites?

106. Holy Sites and Safety

Holy Sites and Safety

So that the holy sites, the Kabah, served by Quraysh can remain safe
Safe in their times of winter and summer
So that everyone can come, visit, worship and do pilgrimage
To this Holy House of God, the Kabah
Who made it worry free of hunger, fear and danger
[106:1–4]

Discussion Questions

1. How do you connect this chapter with the previous one?
2. What has been the current geographical, weather, and financial condition of Makkah where the holy sites are located?
3. Did the holy site, Kabah, face any destruction and turmoil in its history?
4. What is expected with the destruction of Kabah in the prophecy of the Prophet Muhammad?
5. Do Muslims worship the Kabah?
6. What is the significance of Kabah compared to human life in Islamic theology?

107. Being Mindful in Chants and Prayers

Being Mindful in Chants and Prayers

In loss are the chanters, meditators, and worshippers
Who are not mindful, attentive and focused in their engagement
[107:4–5]

Discussion Questions

1. Is it difficult to fully focus during the meditation, chants, and worship? What makes it easy or difficult?
2. Does a prayer without full focus have benefits to the person? Why?

108. The River and Expiration

Indeed, we have given you the river of Kowthar with no expiration
Therefore, appreciate, pray and worship to your Merciful and Caring God
And do your sacrifice for God only

Don't worry about the ones who hate and cause problems for you
Indeed, your hater is the one who is unproductive, self-destructive, and expired
[108:1–3]

Discussion Questions

1. If there are people who hate or cause problems for a person, what is suggested according to the above lines?
2. Is it easy to ignore the mischief or troublemakers? What makes it easier to ignore them?
3. According to the above verse, do the haters hurt themselves? Why and how?

109. Dialogue, Tolerance, and Acceptance

Dialogue, Tolerance, Acceptance

Say: Oh the ones who do not recognize and accept God!
I do not worship and believe in yours and
You do not worship and believe in mine

And You do not worship and believe in mine
And I do not worship and believe in yours and

Your belief and worship is yours and
My belief and worship is mine
[109:1-6]

Commentary

This chapter emphasizes the need for dialogue, tolerance, and acceptance for different people with varying beliefs in a society. Individuals in a community can have differences and may not subscribe to the same norms. However, having mutual respect for each other is critical and necessary for social cohesion.

Discussion Question

1. Do the Muslim societies practice this notion of dialogue, tolerance, and acceptance today? How did they understand this in the past?

110. Victory and Humbleness

Victory and Humbleness

When the help of God and victory comes
When you see people recognizing their Care Giver, God
Becoming content in their relationship with God and
Accepting the true message in abundance

Then, glorify your Real Doer and the Real Cause, God
With full appreciation and full merit and
Increase in abundance your repentance to your Most Merciful God
Indeed, God is very and always Forgiving
[110:1–3]

Commentary

This chapter urges the believers to remember, glorify, and repent to God in the times of personal or group achievements. The verses urge Muslims to seek repentance when successful or victorious, and to avoid any penchant for arrogance.

Discussion Question

1. What is your understanding of the chapter? Do people have a penchant for arrogance after an achievement? How can one prevent self-arrogance in this case?

111. Evil Plots

Plotting and Evil

His wealth, and his struggle for plotting evil
Did not benefit him
[111:2]

Commentary

This short chapter is quite interesting. It refers to family members of the Prophet and how they plotted to harm and hurt him. The only reason for their contempt towards the Prophet was the latter's message of inviting people to believe in the Creator and discouraging them from worshiping idols. The chapter discusses the attitude of an uncle of the Prophet. Prior to the Prophet's prophethood, this uncle was pleased with the Prophet as his nephew. However, as soon as Muhammad started inviting people to Islam, his uncle disavowed him, regarded him as a great enemy, and plotted numerous evils against his once beloved nephew.

Discussion Questions

1. Do family members disown anyone that changes his or her faith? Is it challenging for a person to face pressure from family members during this transition?
2. Is it common to have close family members or intimate friends plot evil against a person? Why?

112. Who is God?

Chapter of Sincerity and Unity

Say:
God is One.
God does not need anything or anyone but everything and everyone needs God.
God does neither have any parents nor any children.
God is Unique, not like any human, not like any creation.
There is no equivalent to God
[112:1-4]

Transliteration from the original scripture:
Qul Huwa Allahu Ahad. Allahu Assamad. Lam Yalid wa lam yuulad. Wa lam yakun lahu kufuwan Ahad.

Commentary

One of the key chapters in the Quran is the chapter of sincerity/unity (Ikhlas). It is a key chapter in establishing a Union with the person and God. Muslims rationalize, experience, and vocalize this chapter in their prayers. They especially expand the understanding of the key expression "La ilaha illa Allah." According to the Prophet Muhammad, this one-line chapter has a value for God almost equivalent to one-third of the full scripture of the Quran. The reason is that this chapter presents the essence of God. Therefore, the Prophet recommends this chapter along with the last two chapters of the Quran to read them three times, blow into the hands, and wipe the hands to the whole body for protection and blessing. This Quranic chapter also has two unique names of God: Samad and Ahad. Samad is a term only used for God. It does not have any popular usage in the language. It generally translates as the One who does not need anything, but everyone and everything needs God. It is also interesting to note that Samadhi as a word is one of the last stages that is attained in Hinduism, Buddhism, and Jainismand Sikhism. In Islam, a person could be denoted as a servant of the Samad.[95]

---

95. As Abdussamad in Ar and it can be used as a name of a person.

Discussion Questions

1. What is the significance of this chapter in Islamic creed?
2. Why is this chapter named as the chapter of unity, or chapter of sincerity?
3. What is the suggested times of reading this chapter according to the practice of the Prophet Muhammad?

113. Day

Day

Chant, Meditate and Say![96]

I take shelter
In God, the Merciful Creator and Watcher of the Day

I take shelter
In God, from the harm of all the creations that God creates

I take shelter
In God, from the harm when night covers with its darkness

I take shelter
In God, from the harm of the self and the persons indulging in evil talismanic powers and black magic[97]

I take shelter
In God, from the harm of persons indulging in jealousy and hatred
[113:1–5]

Discussion Questions

1. Why is there a detailed description of taking shelter or protection from the evil?
2. When do people read this chapter in practice?
3. How many times should a person read this chapter for protection according to the teaching of the Prophet?

---

96. Qul translated as chant, meditate, and say instead of "say" as in literal translations in order to reflect the practiced meanings.
97. Classical translations prefer to use magic which was avoided here. Magic in everyday American language is mostly used to imply something positive rather than its literal meaning.

114. Full Protection

Full Protection

Chant, Meditate and Say!

I ask protection and take shelter
　　In God, the Merciful Creator of the people

I ask protection and take shelter
　　In the True Authority of the people

I ask protection and take shelter
　　In the True Deity of the people

I ask protection and take shelter
In the Merciful Creator, True Authority and True Deity
from all the temptations, and bad thoughts of evildoers
who constantly send evil thoughts and depressions to the chest of the
　　people

I ask protection and take shelter
In the Merciful Creator, True Authority and True Deity
from all the evil of unseen beings, Jinn and humans
[114:1–6]

Discussion Questions

1. What is the significance of this chapter in practice?
2. Why is it critical to ask protection constantly in practice?

PART 3
PREFERRED METHODOLOGY OF TRANSLATION

Most people who practice Islam do not understand Quranic Arabic and rely on colloquial translations of the sacred text. In the English-speaking world, a contemporary translation of a particular passage can have a major impact on behavior and can even encourage social conflict. Each translation has different connotations in the target language. The goal is to minimize the connotations that are not suggested in the original text.

I argue that it is important to include the concerns of contemporary translation methods in the Quranic translations. As an example of this effort, an article on the method of translation of the verses of the Quran by Kumek[36] is presented in the Appendix. In this study, the preferred methodology of translation is to focus on the pragmatic method of Chesterman's[37] taxonomy that would prevail the exegetical meanings in translation. As an example of this preferred methodology for the Quranic verses, the study in the Appendix first reviews the existing popular translations of the verse in the Quran [3:64], often translated, as "a common word among us," then explores the traditional and contemporary exegetical meanings, and finally offers possibilities in translation. The common word verse is selected as an example for the analysis, because this verse has gained recently much public attention in the West for contemporizing the relationships between Muslims, Christians, Jews, and other religions.[38] After reviewing this methodology, one can realize that this book uses this preferred methodology in the selected passages from the Quran as presented in the Appendix.

APPENDIX

PERILS OF TRANSLATION: TEXT AND BEHAVIOR "A COMMON WORD AMONG US" IN THE QURAN [3:64]

Preferred Methodology of Translation

Most people who practice Islam do not understand Quranic Arabic and rely on colloquial translations of the sacred text. In the English-speaking world, a contemporary translation of a particular passage can have a major impact on behavior and can even encourage social conflict. I argue that it is important to include the concerns of contemporary translation methods in the Quranic translations. In this study, I try to focus on the pragmatic method of Chesterman's [37] taxonomy that would prevail the exegetical meanings in translation. As an example of this effort, the current article first reviews the existing popular translations of the verse in the Quran [3:64], often translated, as "a common word among us," then explores the traditional and contemporary exegetical meanings, and finally offers possibilities in translation. This verse has recently gained much public attention in the West for contemporizing the relationships between Muslims, Christians, Jews, and other religions.

Introduction

This chapter is an effort to describe how sacred text can affect behavior in translations. I argue that exegetical translation is vital to reflect the original philological meanings from the source language (SL) of Arabic to the target language (TL) of English. That does not mean that the literal meaning of the verse is not important. The ideal Quranic translation, I think, should prioritize the contextual and philological motifs in the meaning along with semantic and syntactic concerns. Therefore, I will use the words contextual, interpretive, or pragmatic strategies[37] interchangeably in this article to assert the importance of prioritizing and conveying the "message" in the Quranic translations through exegetical meanings.

Recently, there has been considerable attention to the Quranic verses[42] relevant to contemporary social conflicts. Some scholars claimed that particular verses in translations in the English-speaking world promote social conflict and even violence.[43] But many other commentators stress contextual understanding of the verses.[44] Although I fully agree that context and the meaning is crucially important in understanding scriptures, especially through pragmatic methods,[37] and is one of my main arguments in this study; however, I want to untangle another, often untouched, problem in the current literature as well. This is the syntactic and semantic analysis of the English words and phrases chosen in translating the text from the source language of Arabic in order to understand their potential relationship to social conflicts, opposed to unity. Many people who practice Islam do not understand Quranic Arabic but rely on colloquial translations. An incorrect single translated word could divert the reader from the hermeneutical meanings.

As a methodology, I will analyze the available and popular English translations of one of the critical verses in the Quran, named or popularized as "common word." I will review the meanings from the contemporary and traditional exegesis in the literature. Finally, I will present the possible glitches of these available translations and offer possibilities of translations reflecting the equivalence from the source language of Arabic into a contemporary colloquial English. This may offer an alternative that captures unity rather than submerging in verbiage that suggests its opposite.

Translation Theories and the Quran

The purpose of this article is not a substantial indulgence with the translation theories and how it applies to Quranic Arabic. Rather, it is to casually explore and analyze a case of scriptural text (verse) from the source language (SL) of Arabic into the target language (TL) of English by reviewing some of the current available literature. In this perspective, I do not use a top-down approach of using the translation taxonomies and applying it to the text. Rather, I review and assume that current available widely popular translated texts into the target language already has value through text to genre then to discourse then to register which implies rhetorical purpose, communicative event, ideology/perspective, and situationality respectively.[45] Chesterman's[37] taxonomy has already been used to review some of the Quranic divine names to explore some of the translation renderings.[46] Chesterman's translation model has two main groups: comprehension and production strategies. Comprehension strategy uses the examination of source language and full design of translation methods. Production strategy uses the results of comprehension design to transform the text from source to target language. This article uses the production strategy in the methodology of translation of scriptural text. I attempt to use a heuristic approach of translation classification in including three primary groups of production strategy: syntactic/grammatical, semantic, and pragmatic.[37]

SYNTACTIC	SEMANTIC	PRAGMATIC
Literal translation	Synonym	Cultural Filtering
Loan	Antonym	Explicitness
Transposition	Hyponym	Information Change
Unit Shift	Converse	Interpersonal Change
Phrase Structure Change	Abstraction	Illocutionary Change
Clause Structure Change	Distribution	Coherence Change
Sentence Structure Change	Emphasis Change	Partial Translation
Cohesion Change	Paraphrase	Visibility Change
Level Shift		Transediting
Scheme Change		Other Pragramatic Changes

Table 1   Chesterman's (1997) Production Strategies

Below is an outline of the concrete approach of the above three categories.

> If syntactic strategies manipulate form, and semantic strategies manipulate meaning, pragmatic strategies can be said to manipulate the message itself. These strategies are often the result of a translator's global decisions concerning the appropriate way to translate the text as a whole.[37]

In this perspective, I do not aim to nitpick much on syntactic and semantic issues, rather focus on pragmatic concerns or strategies of translation by bringing the conventional Quranic exegetical meanings into translation. In this perspective of reviewing the Quranic exegesis, the stance is translating this text to favor unity rather than discord among the religions. One of the key elements that I strongly believe and understand is the importance of cultural filtering in the taxonomy of pragmatic strategy in the table above by Chesterman[37]. If the naturalization, domestication, or adaptation of the source text is not adapted then exoticization, foreignization, or estrangement occurs.[47] Therefore, I frequently focus on cultural filtering (Chesterman) in the critique of the current translations and will offer possible alternatives.

Common Word

The "common word" in the verse of the Quran, [3:64], has attracted public and academic attention from not only Muslims but also from Christians and Jews. Yale Divinity School held a conference[42]. The Tony Blair Foundation[38] published a book on the topic. News articles appeared on NY Times[48] and BBC[49] focusing on this verse and the phrase "common word."

I argue that the translation of this text of the Quran in the chapter of Family of Imran shows a passage [3:64] calling to unity, a call often submerged in verbiage that suggests its opposite. The available translations of this passage into English seem to be different. These differences or deficiencies relate to the variances between Arabic and English in their syntax, semantics, and pragmatic translation strategies[37] Translations inevitably leave some areas silent. Perforce, "translators are traitors," as the Italian proverb suggests and one can always argue the perspective of loss and gain in translations.[50] These silent connotations, as subtexts, still leave several possible interpretations. In English language, the preference for brevity excludes many possibilities that Quranic Arabic grammar permits and even requires. English favors the simplest narratives and leaves subtext areas dangling or silent. But Arabic suggests multiplicities of allusions and possibilities of interpretation over the text. We need to look at the other contexts of these English words and what they suggest to current readers. In the West, this sort of Quranic analysis is still in an embryonic state.[51]

In this article, I try to center on the contextual exegetical meaning of the verse, *Kalimatin saaw āin baynan ā wa Baynakum*, "a common word among us," in the chapter of Family of Imran, verse 64, which calls Christians, Jews, Muslims, and other religions to a common ground. Analysis of the Quranic expressions—grammatical, idiomatic, metaphoric, stylistic, and contextual—can suggest dialogue among

Christians, Jews, and other religions[54]. One can say that the Quran in this verse urges people not to focus on doctrinal minutiae.

The portion of the verse focused upon in this article transliterates[91] as: Qul! yā ahlul kitā[92] bi (kitaabi)[93] ! ta'alaw ilā kalimatin sawāin, baynanā wa baynakum, alla na'buda illa Allah, wa la nushrika bihi shayan, wa la yattqhizha ba'dunā ba'dan arbaban min dūni Allahi. Fain tawallaw, faqūlū: ashadū biannā muslimūn.

The purpose of this article is not to suggest liberal expressions of the text of the Quranic verse but rather to review and interpret or translate the orthodox and linguistic approaches such as in the works of traditional scholars such as Al Jurjani,[94] or Zamahshari[95] to the language of contemporary time with the equivalence methodologies of translation as much as possible. Among the many factors of Quranic translation, morphological, epistemological, grammatical, idiomatic, metaphoric, stylistic, technical, and contextual (urf), apparent (lafzi) and hidden (ishari) meanings are important to distinguish.[52] In addition, there is a strong relationship between the translator and the translated text.

Mustansir Mir's literal analysis of the Quran, the Quran as literature[53][54] analyzes Quranic speech using linguistic concepts such as asyndeton, polysyndeton, parallelism, chiasmus, and "envelope." Toorawa[51] emphasizes the importance of showing an effort to conserve the original rhyme structure of the Quran when translated to English. Abu Zayd[55] in his article outlines the problem of sole literary approach to understand the message of the Quran.

---

91. Transliteration is a dictation or writing of the words from one language with different alphabet to another language through hearing. For example, one can encounter in writings "qul" or "kul" in transliteration of the same word, قل, from Arabic to English due to the expression of the similar sounds in English.
92. Arabic word structure requires correct elongation with each letter of a word. An incorrect more or less elongation of a letter for a word can change the meaning of it.
93. According to the widely-used Arabic transliteration scheme[56], to denote elongations in the transliterated text instead of writing kitābi, kitābi could be used.
94. Al Jurjani lived during the eleventh century. He was a famous Arabic linguistic specializing in Quranic eloquence, rhetoric, and metaphor.
95. Zamakshari was an Arabic linguist who lived between the eleventh and twelfth century. His book, Al-Kashhaaf, is one of the most famous Quranic linguistic commentaries.

Previous Translations and Their Glitches

Below are the different translations of the verse [3:64] in some of the most popular English interpreted Qurans. In the translation of Usmani,[96] the verse reads[3]:

> Say, O people of the Book, come to a word common between us and between you, that we worship none but Allah, that we associate nothing with Him and that some of us do not take others as lords instead of Allah. Then, should they turn back, say: "Bear witness that we are Muslims." [3:64]

This translation uses contemporary English including literal and exegetical meanings. I believe it misses idiomatic and metaphorical meanings; for example, using "turn back" instead of "turn away" for the meaning of rejection. "Turn back" suggests physically moving in the opposite direction whereas "turning away" suggests avoiding or rejecting an idea. Analyzing this translation through Chesterman's [37] taxonomy, phrase structure change in syntax leads to emphasis change in semantics and this leads to cultural filtering problem in pragmatic strategy of translation.

Yusuf Ali's[97][5] popular English translation, which also uses "turn back," reads:

> Say: "O People of the Book! Come to common terms as between us and you: That we worship none but Allah; that we associate no partners with him; that we erect not, from among ourselves, Lords and patrons other than Allah." If then they turn back, say ye: "Bear witness that we (at least) are Muslims (bowing to Allah's Will) [3:64].

Yusuf Ali's translation is one of the early English renderings, which makes it difficult for today's reader to understand the archaic language. Sometimes archaic language can cause abstraction in semantics.[37] This may lead to visibility change and explicitness in meaning.[37] This translation has the similar issue of the phrase "turn back" as mentioned above.

---

96. Mufti Taqi Usmani is a well-known legal Islamic scholar, born in Pakistan, who is closely working with the contemporary issues of Muslims, including those living in the West.
97. Yusuf Ali's English translation has been one of the first and most widespread one used in the West.

Arthur John Arberry[63] was a British Muslim journalist who worked at Cairo University as the department chair of Classics, translates[98] this verse [3:64], thus:

> Say: 'Oh! People of the Book! Come now to a word common between us and you, that we serve none but God, and that we associate not aught with Him, and do not some of us take others as lords, apart from God.' And if they turn their backs, say: 'Bear witness that we are Muslims.' [3:64]

Arberry's adaptation captures the meaning, but the language suffers from his coy archaisms like "aught with." He uses "turn their backs," implying hostility perhaps even greater than "turn back."

Saheeh International,[23] by a group of scholars in S. Arabia translate the verse as:

> Say, "O People of the Scripture, Come to a word that is equitable between us and you—that we will not worship except Allah and not associate anything with Him and not take one another as lords instead of Allah." But if they turn away, then say, "Bear witness that we are Muslims [submitting to Him]. [3:64]

The Saheeh International translation group comprises Western-born scholars. Although they understand the contextual meaning, using "turn away" instead of "turn back" in the above verse, they use a legalism such as "equitable" in the case of *sawāin* rather than a more inclusive phrase. "Equitable" is a legalistic term implying potential conflict and adjudication. Syntactically, this translation inclines to literal translation which may cause the issues of cultural filtering and information change in pragmatic meaning[37].

Muhammad Pickthall was a Christian-born British Muslim thinker. Pickthall's translation[4], standard in the English world, reads:

---

98. The Quran is in Arabic. Islamic scholars do not consider the translations of the Quran as the original revealed text but close meanings with possible interpretations. Therefore, in Muslim tradition mere translation of the Quran is recommended with some commentaries. Thus, Pickthall's title is, for example, "The meanings of the glorious Quran." This could help the reader to understand the context and essence of the message.

Say: O People of the Scripture! Come to an agreement between you and us: that we shall worship none but Allah, and that we shall ascribe no partner unto Him, and that none of us shall take others for lords beside Allah. And if they turn away, then say: Bear witness that we are they who have surrendered (unto Him). [3:64]

Muhammad Asad was a Jewish-born Austro-Hungarian Islamic thinker who became Muslim in 1926 in Berlin. His translation reads[13]:

Say: O followers of earlier revelation! Come unto that tenet which we and you hold in common: that we shall worship none but God, and that we shall not ascribe divinity to aught beside Him, and that we shall not take human beings for our lords beside God." And if they turn away, then say: "Bear witness that it is we who have surrendered ourselves unto Him" [3:64].

Due to the differences between English and Arabic, the choice of words in translation is critical. Sometimes the choice of a wrong single word in a verse could give unusual sub-textual meanings in English. This may lead to major non-contextual interpretations of the entire verse. Both Pickthall and Asad used a mixture of idiomatic and archaic styles, which led to the problems of abstraction in semantics and lack of explicitness in the pragmatic strategy of Chesterman's [37] categorization. However, their apparent disadvantage for the American reader is their affinity for the British style, such as preference of "shall" over present-day usages of "will" or "should," depending on the meaning in American English.

Quranic Pragmatic Strategy

The Quran itself uses pragmatic strategies in different locations not to convey a single message but contextualizes the meaning through cultural filtering.[37] The Quran accepts the differences but emphasizes the commonalities between these three religions, Islam, Christianity, and Judaism. One of the main commonality is that each religion has its own scripture from God. Muslims are holders of the Quran. Jews are holders of the Tanach, which includes the Torah. Christians are holders of the Bible. Quran urges its followers to establish a common ground as "Peoples of the Book" among the religions with divine scripture. "Peoples of the Book" in the orthodox exegesis of the Quran includes Christians and Jews. The Quran asks Muslims, as the followers of a divine scripture, to establish a common identity with followers of different but kindred divine scriptures, such as Christians and Jews.

Quranic figures of speech have commonalities with Biblical figures of speech. In his article, Mir shows the distinctive features of Quranic dialogue among different parties. Mir[53] says:

> There are, for example, no folk songs in the Quran, no elegies and lamentations, no prophetic rhapsodies, no idyllic poems, and certainly no acrostic. On the other hand, the Quran possesses a rich literary repertoire of its own. Besides making a masterful use of language on the level of words and phrases, it contains figures of speech, satire, and irony; employs a variety of narrative and dramatic techniques; and presents characters that, is (sic.) spite of the sparse personal detail provided about them, come across as vivid figures. For those who can read the Quran in Arabic, the all-pervading rhythm which, in conjunction with the sustained use of what may be called rhymed prose, creates in many Surahs a spellbinding effect that is impossible to reproduce. There is the characteristic terseness of the Quranic language which makes for some complex constructions, but which it is difficult to convey in English without being awkward. (52)

The Quran invites readers not to denounce unbelievers but to examine them carefully[53]. The underlying assumption is that non-Muslims can appreciate the merit, eloquence, and beauty of the Quran.

Mir divides Quranic dialogues into several types. Some are between the prophets and the nation to which the message was sent. Others are between God and prophets, or among humans both in the world and the hereafter, or one-sided dialogues (monologues).

This paper suggests an additional dialogue in the Quran between Muslims and People of the Book. This dialogue sometimes arises from their questioning with the expression, *yasal ūnaka*. The phrase *yasal ūnaka* translates as "they are asking." Here, "they" are sometimes Jews, Christians, or Meccan pagans. God tells Muhammad how to respond to them. Sometimes God reminds Muhammad that there is a similar order in the Bible: the Gospel, the Psalms, and the Torah as in the Quran that they should follow. One of the obvious ones is that "killing an innocent human being is equivalent to killing all humanity" as mentioned in the Quran [5:32] and Talmud, in Mishnah Sanhedrin [4:5] and Babylonian Talmud Tractate Sanhedrin [37a]. Sometimes the Quran gives the response directly without entertaining the historical perspectives. For example, Jews in Madina ask about the nature of the soul or spirit (*yasal ūnaka anil ruh...*) and the response is that it is an "order from my Lord." [17:85] (i.e., God only knows it's real nature).

In the case of Surah Āl'i I'mrān,[99] in the verse [3:64]

> Say, O people of the Book, Come to a word common between us and between you (emphasis added by bolding the text), that we worship none but Allah, that we associate nothing with Him and that some of us do not take others as Lords instead of Allah. Then, should they turn back, say: "Bear witness that we are Muslims."[3]

God orders the prophet Muhammad to be in communication with the other people of the Book, Christians and Jews. God also teaches the prophet and Muslims what the essence of the dialogue should be. The Quran suggests that a reminder and open communication that belief of the same God or the Creator should set the tone. This commonality should be the "common word" or belief shared before embarking upon further discourse.

Quranic language could be analyzed through meaning, grammar, idioms, metaphors, style, and context. For example, Quranic language uses different metaphors to depict certain occasions to picture vividly

---

99. Āl'i I'mrān is the name of the chapter of the Quran. Quran chapters are denoted either by the name of the chapter or by a number. This is the fourth chapter of the Quran that explains about Āl'i I'mrān. Āl'i I'mrān literally translates as the "Family of Imran." I'mrān is the father of Mary who is the mother of Jesus. Imran's wife makes a sincere prayer to God to have a child to dedicate him for God's path. As a result of this prayer, God gives her Mary. Mary, as a pious woman, dedicates her entire life worshipping God in the temple. According to the Quran, God gives Mary a son, Jesus, a Prophet of God and a Messiah.

and lively a possible future and past panorama. Quranic grammar sometimes uses very complex structures, incorporating very rich stylistic language and dialogue. It deliberately chooses where to use active and passive tense, length of sentences (*itnāb*—explanatory sentences, *musāwi*—one-to-one correspondence, and *ijāz*—concise structure) and language registrars in syntactic and semantic strategies.[37]

Review and Analysis of the Exegetical Meanings

This section reviews and analyzes some of the traditional and contemporary exegetical meanings of this verse of the Quran in order to cognize the depiction of the idealized relationship of Muslims with other religions. The aim of this section is to ultimately represent these exegetical meanings of the verse in the translations. Fakhr al-Din al-Razi[57], a prominent medieval commentator and theologian, suggests three possible referents of the phrase *ahlul kitab*, "People of the Book." The first are the Christians of Najran, where the Prophet hosted them in his own mosque and encouraged them to perform their own Christian worship. The second possibility is the Jews of the Madina. The third possibility is both. Razi[57] emphasizes that the expression "people of the book" itself demonstrates respect for Christians and Jews. He says that it is a similar expression when someone makes a factual statement about another person. For example, a person is holding the entire Quran in his memory and he is called a *hafizul Quran*, "the holder of Quran" or "the memorizer of the Quran." The phrase "people of the book" is an honorific, like the phrase *hafizul quran* for a person who has memorized the Quran, a title of respect. In Muslim tradition, if someone is called *hafizul quran*, it is a dignity expression similar to calling someone Dr. (holds a degree of doctorate). This title is put in front of the person's name in all types of communication. Similarly, the Quran calls and teaches Muslims to address Christians and Jews or whoever received a book from God with an honorary salutation[57]. Especially in eastern cultures, honor and respect has a deeper meaning beyond its usage as a formal salutation.

Ta'alaw is a respectful phrase for gaining the listener's attention. *Kalimah* literally translated as "word" or a "statement" signifies a bridge between

Muslims and "people of the book" according to Fakhr al-Din al-Razi.[57]

Sawāin could be literally translated as "common," "equal," and/or "share," and so forth. Fakhr al-Din al-Razi analyzes the word *insaf* from *nisf* (half) like *sawāin*. When something is equally shared into two halves (e.g., half for Muslims and the other share among the people of the book), bringing them together produces completeness and balance. [If only one owns half then it will be incomplete and possibly darkness and oppression.] Baghawi[100] (1987, first published circ. 1120) and other commentators especially emphasize the meaning of the *sawaun* as the judicial bond between us and them or the teachings that are common among different groups.

The Quran, with the expression *sawāin*, suggests that despite diverse ethno-religious labeling Jewish and Christian sacred texts and teachings have an essence, which they share with Islam.

This paper glosses *baynanā as* "among Muslims" in this verse. *Baynanā* is literally and contextually translated as "among Muslims" in this verse according to the normative exegesis of the Quran. This word implies that there could be a special education to implant this approach of commonality. On the other hand, *baynakum* is normatively translated as "Christians, Jews, Hindus, etc. . . ." This expression may refer to different religions through the agent of the scripture that was revealed.

The translation of the Quran by Yildirim,[44] suggests that the Quran invites Christians first because there are so many of them compared to followers of other religions. It invites all the other religions after. Yildirim says that the Quran shows how different races, religions, nations, or ethnic groups can agree and unite on common values, such as the legal right of freedom. M. Wahid Khan[58] comments that although the Quran criticizes the editorial deviations of the Old and New Testaments from the originals one can still incorporate the "commonality" of monotheism that serves as the ground for the unification. Some others[25] expand on this concept of commonality with the idea that we are all creatures but not inanimate like stones or soil. We are not plants. We are not lower animals. We are all humans. We share the same earth, air, water, food, and so forth. We have similar weaknesses and

---

100. Baghawi is a prominent Islamic textual medieval commentator and theologian, d.1122.

worries. We have the same Creator. So if this unity is one, then why do we concentrate on our minute differences?

According to Sabuni,[59] *sawāin* means *adl* in Arabic, which translates as justice. Reading this way, the Quran is calling all Christians, Jews, and Muslims to form a common ground, society, or a community on the basis of "Justice." Looking at the verses before and after this verse, this justice is first knowing God, His existence, uniqueness, and unity and building common grounds from there. Like Sabuni, Ibn Kathir (medieval expert on Quranic exegesis, died 1373)[60] glosses *sawāin* as *adl*, "justice" and "mercy," *nasf (ar.)*. Thus, *sawāin* connotes as justice, human rights, no superiority of one above another (*wal yattahizu ba'dunā ba'dan arbaba*), shared values, and unification under the umbrella of believing in one Creator. If one side has half and the other has nothing, the resulting imbalance is intrinsically unjust.

Through the recitational interpretation of the Quran, the Quranic words have internal rhythm (i.e., Musiki, Turk.) among the words. The letters that compose the word, the words that compose the sentences (verses), and the sentences that compose the chapters all have an internal rhythm and beat that either paint or echo (or both) the contextual meaning in the Quran. Even the sound of elongated words in the grammatical context is another point of emphasis. In Arabic, not all the words have elongation. *Sawāin* has an elongation (*mad*) in its recitation on the vowels of *ā* or "aa" according to recitation (*tajwēd*) rules of the Quran. In this verse, *sawāin*, "common," with the elongation in *ā* or "aa" suggests that there are a lot of commonalities. As an example, if we elongate the word a "lot" as if it reads in English as a "Loooot" of commonalities as does *sawaaaain* in its proper Arabic *tajwēd*. Elongation could imply the numerous or extended or many common values of Islam, Christianity, and Judaism.

The Quran stresses that accepting the monotheism must be voluntary, not forced as mentioned in the verse [2:256] "there is no compulsion (force) in the religion." In other words, it is illegal in Islamic law and tradition to force someone to change her/his religion. Therefore, if people don't accept the common ground of *sawāin* voluntarily, coercion is out of the question. People are free to choose what they want to believe and what they want to do.

The Quran repeats and highlights the concept of transgression or wrong (*zulm*). Transgression (wrong) comes in two types: one is against the Creator and the other is against the people. Transgression against the Creator does not bear any earthly accountability.[101] This transgression is mainly not recognizing Him as the Creator and consequently not appreciating His favors. The second type of transgression is against human dignity or social justice. It could involve invidious discrimination by race, ethnicity, or religion. The Quran suggests legal measures to eliminate this type of transgression. Some social Islamic scholars, such as Fazlur Rahman, [33] suggest that this law enforcement could be secular as long as the laws are fair, just, and, transparent which is the essential objective of the Quranic legal system (*sharia*).

As the result of both types of offenses, according to Quranic teachings, *wa lakinna anfusahum yazlimūn*, "the person in reality wrongs (oppresses or transgresses) himself." Therefore, in the later part of the verse discussed [3:64], after the invitation to a common word (the same Creator) the verse ends as "And if they turn away, say: 'Bear witness that we are Muslims.'" It reminds Muslims that if their invitation is not accepted or welcomed, one can tell them that we will still submit ourselves to our Lord's order.

The Core: Kalimah—A Word

In the remaining portion of the verse, the Quran instructs that there is a word, a value, or a theme for what Muslims, Christians, and Jews know and agree, *kalimah*. The Quran instructs that Christians, Muslims, and Jews all pledge to God to believe in Him and worship and please Him. As it says in Deuteronomy [6:4]: "Hear, O Israel: The Lord our God, the Lord is one." According to R. Marston Speight[61], Christ and his followers make the divine attribute of unity central to Christian theology. So this common word is with this recognition, accepting that no human is superior to another on religious grounds.

---

101. If the person does not believe in God this is a major transgression against the right of God in Islam. Transgression is due to not appreciating and recognizing the Creator. This type of transgression does not entail any type of punishment in the world. Therefore, according to the Islamic creed, one could see people who do not believe in God but may enjoy abundant bounties from God. Their transgression toward God will be addressed in the Hereafter. The punishment and reward will be in full effect over there.

The basic common ground suggested by the Quran offers a way for humans to live together peacefully even though they may not share the same beliefs, practices, cultures, or ethnicities. A fundamental Quranic principle is that there is no compulsion in religion [2:255]. Muslims should build religious toleration by accommodating different faiths other their own [109:1–5]. This teaching provides a platform for people with different beliefs or unbelievers. Due to this teaching, non-Muslim ancient religions and communities were safe in Muslim lands, for example during the Abbasid, Umayyad, or Ottoman era, for centuries.

Many scholars explain the *kalimah* in the verse as the acceptance of one common Creator. The analogy could be that when there is a problem among the children, they go to their father to solve it for them. Similarly, the problems that humans face today could be solvable by the teachings of the Creator. There are common teachings in the sacred texts of the Creator. For example, stealing, lying, killing an innocent person, and backbiting are all sins in Judaism, Christianity, and Islam and also for most of the other religions. Being truthful, helping the poor and one's neighbors, and using good words are virtues in these religions. Taking a common God or Creator as the problem-solver suggests the ability and affinity to discuss social problems. As suggested,[62] practical implication of having the understanding of the common God between Jews, Christians, and Muslims could "move us all forward with common purpose, rather than act as a wedge that only drives us further apart." This could build avenues for potential solutions of the conflicts among these religions.

However, one may bring the question, for example, of abortion or other issues around which these three Abrahamic religions have similar teachings which modern secularists reject. The Quran emphasizes the personal free choice. God makes the best and just contextual and circumstantial judgment for His creation with His mercy according to the Quran.

In the Quranic understanding of *kalimah*, knowing God's name is not as important as His correctly understanding His attributes. As mentioned in [17:110]: "Say: Call upon God (Allah), or call upon the Merciful (Ar-Rahman); whichever you call upon, to Him belong the Names Most Beautiful . . . " This may suggest that the Creator could be called

God, Lord, Allah, Adonai, Elohim, Yahweh, Universal Intelligence, or Brahma[102] as long as it means or implies one of the beautiful and perfect names of the Creator.

Furthermore, in referring to the Creator, God's correct understanding and true attributes are essential according to the Quran. For example, the pagans during the time of the Prophet Muhammad called the Creator with the proper Islamic name, Allah. But, the monotheistic understanding of God was not there. Allah was one god among many. The Quran educates them by asking critical questions. It asks [23:84-85]: Say: "Whose is the earth, and who is in it, if you have knowledge?"[63] They say, God's (Allah's). "Say: 'Will you not then remember?'" The Quran asks the pagans again [23:86-87]: "Say: who is the Lord of the seven heavens and the Lord of the mighty Throne? They say, 'God's (Allah's). Say: Will you not then be God-fearing?"[653] These questions are to lead idolaters to reflect on their understanding of God. The pagans believe in God (Creator) and at the same time, they believe in different idols as gods. Here, the Quranic style is pushing them to rethink their henotheism so that they do not associate any partners with Him. The common grounds could be expanded to commonalities such as love, ethics, and accountability.

The Quran urges people not to focus on doctrinal minutiae. The following verse of the Quran again in the Chapter of Family of Imran [3:65] gives Prophet Abraham as the example of practicing this common word although there is a dispute about the religion to which he belongs. The Quran emphasizes the importance of leaving this inessential argument of group "ownership" of Abraham. Rather, it asks the followers of three religions to concentrate on the essence of his message of beliefs and values.

Finally, the Quran does not avoid demonstrating the differences of beliefs or values. It vividly contrasts the differences in multiple occasions. For example, in the immediate previous verses [3:59-63] right before the

---

102. In Islamic creed, correct understanding of the Creator with His proper name is Allah. All the best and beautiful names in its perfectness belong to Allah. These names and attributes of the Creator, Allah, are in the Quran and in the sayings of the Prophet Muhammad. There is a substantial opinion among the scholars of Islamic creed that calling or referring to Allah with the attributes and names other than the Quranic ones could be problematic.

discussion of the verse of this article [3:64], it points out the difference of the belief between Christians and Muslims on Jesus. For example [3:59–60]:

> For (the Creator) God, Jesus's creation is similar to creation of Adam. (Adam was both without father and mother). God created Adam from mud, God said "Be" and Adam was created. The truth is from your Lord. You unquestionably should not have any doubt about it. (my trans.)

The above verse indicates that if God created Adam without any father and mother, God certainly can create Jesus without any mother. Adam was not divine and so Jesus was not divine according to the Quran. But then, it directs or advises on a possible methodology that dialogue and communication start with common and shared values rather than pointing out these conflicts. The Quran then suggests that a possible source of dialogue among these three religions could be the values of Abraham. It shows a path in order not to be obstructed by mere ignorant "ownership" arguments among the followers of different religions about the teachings of Abraham. But, rather it suggests that the focus should be on the essence of his message that he symbolized straightforwardness and believing in one God.

One other possibility of Kalimah, the word, could be Jesus himself. This argument has a place in both Muslim and Christian resources.[64] When Jesus's miraculous birth and immaculate conception was explained in the Quran, Kalimah is used [4:171]. On the other hand, in Christian sources, word of God (logos) is a common approach to explain the birth of Jesus.[65] In this case, the meaning of the verse can emphasize the commonalities shared among Muslims and Christians could be Jesus and his teachings.

It seems irrational and unnatural, as some of the post and neo-orientalists assert,[43] to interpret obvious commonalities of Christianity, Judaism, and Islam as diverging points and not as common traits, since the obvious commonalities among all Abrahamic religions are very vivid and almost need no interpretation.[103]

Recently, some scholars[38] interpreted *kalimah*, "Common Word" as the "love of God" and "love of your neighbor." "Love your neighbor" interpretation included as all the humanity regardless of their faith or ethnic tradition. Jifri[38] mentions that God has sent books to solve human problems, but religions become part of the problem. According to him, God creates beauty, and humans love beauty; therefore, they should love God. Humans have a tendency to love the one who is benevolent. This type of love implies a natural love toward the Creator. People cannot generally choose their "neighbors." A person may change his house but how about his town, his city, country, or planet? Jifri[38] interprets this as the choice of God, that you should love your neighbor even though your neighbor may not be a pleasant person, as in the traditional Muslim example of the famous Jurist, Imam Abu Hanifa's relationship with his neighbor.[104] In a global scale, a person's neighbor may be of a different color, ethnicity, or religion. Understanding and interpreting this common word, *kalimah*, becomes more critical. Syed Husain Nasr (Volf[38]) summarizes the classical approaches and suggests similarities about the understanding of God, and its universal teachings among Islam, Christianity, and Judaism. He harshly criticizes the teaching or vulgarization of a separate God[105] among Abrahamic traditions.

---

103. I think Crone[43] takes a deliberate stance to distance Christianity from Islam. Her analysis of the Quranic stories interestingly reads the commonalities as conflicts. It seems that she is not focusing on the literal text but commentaries.
104. Imam Abu Hanifa lived between 699 and 767. His legal teachings are popular in Muslim societies. He was also a devout worshipper of God. He had a neighbor who used to drink and sing loudly all night, disturbing Imam Abu Hanifa during his worship. Due to the strong emphasis to neighborly rights in Islamic jurisprudence, Abu Hanifa put up with his neighbor for many years. One day, he did not hear any noise from his neighbor and investigated the situation immediately. He found that the police had arrested him. He went to the police and bailed him out. As his neighbor witnessed this, he was perplexed and ashamed of himself and stopped drinking and became a pious disciple of God.
105. An Evangelist institute argued that Muslims and Christians have a separate God. Sayyid Hussain Nasr brings an example from Coptic Arab Christians in Egypt that they call God Allah, exactly the same as the Muslim phrase. Allah is the same word for the proper name of the Creator. The first verse of Genesis [1:1] in the Arabic Bible is "Allah created the heavens and the earth."

Some Sufis such as Rumi interpret the common word as any human being with any belief. Rumi[106] [66] illustrates this in his motif:

> Come, come, whoever you are.
> Wanderer, worshipper, lover of living, it doesn't matter
> Ours is not a caravan of despair.
> Come even if you have broken your vow a thousand times,
> Come, yet again, come, come (151).

Possibilities in Genres Reflected in Translations

After the above analysis, to emphasize the contextual insinuations or pragmatic methods,[37] I will present some possibilities of translations from SL to TL. I primarily use the cultural filtering method[37] by considering orthodox and contemporary exegetical meanings. Subsequently, I will review the possible different syntactic and semantic meanings of each word or phrase and insert it in the passage. The tags for each possible different passage will be Aa, Ab, Ac, Ba, and Bc. In these possible translations, the differences are compared to the main translation Aa. In each case, the whole verse is presented. It is purposeful to not only present the difference for the meanings. In normative scholarly and legal interpretations and exegesis of the Quran, contextual (*siyāq and sibāq*[107]) understandings of the verses are paramount.[67]

The phrase *qul*, "say," is used to mean to inform, communicate, notify, or to announce. Therefore, it will be more clear to use the verb inform as hyponym[108] in semantics[37] with its exegetical meaning although the literal translation of *qul* is "say" as most of the translations preferred. "Say" means to utter words[68] in the colloquial English language. Here, the *siyāq and sibāq* in the Quranic exegesis suggest that *qul* does not have a "passive" stand of uttering words but rather informing and communicating with the other scripture followers. This is a very vivid example of cultural filtering in pragmatic strategy of translation.[37]

---

106. Jalal Ad-Din Rumi is a poet, theologian, and mystic scholar who lived in current Afghanistan, Iran, and Turkey between 1200–1273. His poems are translated to English and have gained universal popularity.
107. Siyāq and sibāq are terms to indicate the methodology in the Quranic exegesis for understanding the contextual meaning of the analyzed verse by examining the prior and following verses.
108. Hyponym ensures in semantics a specific meaning rather than a general meaning.

APPENDIX   Perils of Translation

The expression *yā*, is a verbal exclamation mark, like "oh!" in English. One does not commonly and contemporarily use "oh!" unless in an informal conversation, as for example, "Oh My God." In the verse, God uses *yā*, "oh!" to focus attention on an important message. *Yā* could perhaps mean exegetically "please pay attention!" to something "astonishing" or "amazing" that follows. With the exegetical meanings, there is a unit shift of an exclamation to a phrase in syntax[37] and how this could be a cultural filtering issue from SL to TL.

Ahlal kitab literally translates as the people of the book. The connotation is that God revealed earlier scriptures so that the Prophet Muhammad and all Muslims recognize and accept them. In English, there is no phrase as "people of the Book" unless it is a Muslim audience. So, one can prefer to use hyponym and abstraction in semantics to translate this expression as "followers of earlier revelation."[13]

Ta'alaw literally translates as "come." In the verse, it implies calling parties together to resolve a dispute. It is an invitation to suggest a solution to an issue that could lead to puzzlement or argument as mentioned in the verses of the Quran [3:61], [3:64], [3:167], and [6:151]. Therefore, instead of using the literal translation, "Let's get together and discuss or realize," seems a better gloss which includes unit change in syntax; paraphrase, and emphasis change in semantics and cultural filtering and information change in pragmatic method of translation.[37]

Coming to the complex part of the discussion, *Kalimatin sawāin* is translated as "a common word" as presented below in translation "Aa," "a word common,"[3][63] "common terms,"[5] "a word that is equitable,"[23] "an agreement"[4], and "tenet which we and you hold in common."[13] In these renderings, some prefer to use literal translation, transposition, and unit shift in syntax; some use hyponym, emphasis change, and paraphrase in semantics, and some use cultural filtering, partial translation, and explicitness in pragmatic methodology.[37] *Kalimatin sawāin* is mentioned as a singular indefinite article (*nakirah*), which may imply the commonalities could be many and should be realized instead of having a definite article of *al kalimatu assawāu*. The remaining portion of the verse suggests, for this common word, realizing the common Creator and not to worship anything except God. Therefore, Yusuf Ali translated it as "common terms" in plural with the cultural filtering and replacing the general word, "term," with "values" as hyponym. Combining Ali's and Asad's translation, a possible translation for "kalimatin *sawāin*" is "values which we and you hold in common" as presented below in "Ac." Then, we clarify that in this commonness one of the significant one is "worshipping the same creator" by adding the expression "among" them as unit shift in syntax. Such glosses reflect the polysemy of a word like *kalimatin*. A word in English means "a single distinct meaningful element of speech,"[68] although *kalimatin* translates literally as "word." For the context of the passage of the verse [3:64], it holds the meanings of value and theme. Therefore, in different presentations of translations, I use for the translation of the word *kalimatin*, value or theme.

Sawāin stems from an Arabic root word and usually glosses as "justice" and "fairness." We can see this glossing in "Ab" presented below.

Translation "Aa" below is the closest literal translation that could be given with the exegetical meanings. I analyze the verse in three parts. The first part consists of Aa, Ab, Ac, Ba, and Bb, which have possible different translations of the same part of the verse. I treat the second part of the verse after the first part.

> Aa)
> Inform All Christians and Jews and other followers of a Scripture about this Amazing Fact!
> Please Pay Attention Followers of the Earlier Revelations!
> Let's get together and realize a common word between you and us.
> This common word is not to worship anything except our same and common Creator.
>
> Ab)
> Inform All Christians and Jews and other followers of a Scripture about this Amazing Fact!
> Please Pay Attention Followers of the Earlier Revelations!
> Let's get together and realize a common *and just* theme between you and us.
> This common word is not to worship anything except our same and common Creator.

Ac)
Inform All Christians and Jews and other followers of a Scripture about this Amazing Fact!
Please Pay Attention Followers of the Earlier Revelations!
Let's get together and realize the values that we, and you hold in common.
Among these values, primarily, is not to worship anything except our same and common Creator.

Here, "Ac" is the preferred translation for our analysis when we combine exegetical meanings.

If we abbreviate the translation of the verse it reads as: This common word, value, or theme is that we worship the same God. This common theme is that we only worship God. With the more interpretive meanings the verse could possibly read: This common value is the love of God. This common theme is the justice.

In normative Quranic exegesis, the prophet Muhammad is an agent to carry the message from God to people like other messengers. Still, in most of the phrases when Allah says in the Quran "Say" (Qul), the addressee is actually all believers (Muslims). In other words, Muhammad Iqbal stresses[69] that a person should read the Quran as if it was revealed to the reader not to the Prophet Muhammad.

If we take into account cultural filtering in a pragmatic approach,[37] the verse reads as:

Ba)
A scripture from God to the Messenger:
My dear Beloved Messenger Muhammad,
Tell the Believers (Muslims)
To Inform All Christians and Jews and other followers of a Scripture about this Amazing Fact!
Please Pay Attention!
Let's get together and realize common and just values among us.
This common word among us is not to worship anything except our same and common Creator.

Another possible gloss emerges from the conventional and contemporary linguistic analysis of the words under discussion:

> Bb)
> A scripture from God to the Messenger:
> My dear Beloved Messenger Muhammad,
> Tell to the Believers (Muslims)
> To Inform all the Christians and Jews and other followers of a Scripture about this Amazing Fact!
> Please Pay Attention!
> Let's agree on the universal human values to live together on the earth peacefully.
> This common value among us is not to worship anything except our same and common Creator.

The second portion of the verse could continue in different translations as presented in Taqi Usmani's[3]:

> That we worship none but Allah, that we associate nothing with Him and that some of us do not take others as lords instead of Allah.

In Yusuf Ali's translation,[5]

> That we worship none but Allah; that we associate no partners with him; that we erect not, from among ourselves, lords and patrons other than Allah.

In Arberry's translation:

> That we serve none but God, and that we associate not aught with Him, and do not some of us take others as lords, apart from God.

In Saheeh International:

> That we will not worship except Allah and not associate anything with Him and not take one another as lords instead of Allah.

In Pickthall:

> That we shall worship none but Allah, and that we shall ascribe no partner unto Him, and that none of us shall take others for lords beside Allah.

Finally, in Asad's:

> That we shall worship none but God, and that we shall not ascribe divinity to aught beside Him, and that we shall not take human beings for our lords beside God.

All the translators above seem to be in agreement that the main notion is to realize and accept our common Creator, Allah (God). Then, the remaining part of the verse emphasizes the pure monotheism to explain what it means by a common Creator. The first condition is to accept only God as the Creator. It is to worship nothing but God. Some of the above translations use "partner." In English, the word "partnership" has generally positive or constructive meaning. Here, a negative or critical meaning is intended in the SL. The first possible meaning is that a purposeful and explicit or implicit "division" or "split" in the pure belief in the one divine Creator is a conceivable problem. The second possible meaning is that assuming the words of other humans as the words of God is a problem. This could be implicit and mentioned later in the verse because people generally do not take other humans as their Lords, at least in our contemporary time, explicitly. One should remember that there were the cases of kings or pharaoh in the past who had the claims of having divine attributes. There is the emphasis that God does not have any coequals or partners. Neither can divine pharaohs or god kings compete with God's authority. Considering exegetical meanings, "except" is a better word in our TL of contemporary English as used in Saheeh International.

In the beginning of the verse, God calls different groups to make an agreement. Legal language ideally should have "shall," as used in the translations of Pickthall and Asad. "Shall" suggests both future and necessity. I think both Pickthall and Asad translations reflect British usage, in which "shall" is common as American English prefers "will." This brings the visibility change in TL for pragmatic methods.[37]

With the contextual (*siyāq-sibāq*) meaning each "waw" has different meanings. With this, the preferred translation for the portion of the verse could be:

> That we should not worship anything except Allah. This is because we should not ascribe any equal with God. And therefore, we should not consider human beings as divine. We believe that only God is divine.

Alternatively, by considering English language's preference for brevity, simplicity, and abstraction in semantics,[37] we could change the above first part of the verse as in the sentence below, as the TL still could have space for the meaning:

> That we worship only to God. This is because we should not ascribe any equal with God. And therefore, we should not consider human beings as divine. We believe that only God is divine.

Final and third part of the verse is, in Usmani:

> Then, should they turn back, say: "Bear witness that we are Muslims." [3:64]

Yusuf Ali glosses:

> If then they turn back, say ye: "Bear witness that we (at least) are Muslims (bowing to Allah's will)."

Arberry glosses:

> And if they turn their backs, say: "Bear witness that we are Muslims." [3:64]

In Saheeh International it is:

> But if they turn away, then say, "Bear witness that we are Muslims [submitting to Him]."

APPENDIX Perils of Translation

In Asad's translation:

> And if they turn away, then say: "Bear witness that it is we who have surrendered ourselves unto Him."

As I take the objective of cultural filtering and information change[37] through exegetical meanings, "Muslim" could not be in its literal meaning. If a person has all the qualities of believing and worshipping in one God purely and not making others as his or her Lord, then that person is a "Muslim" although they may not be literally called "Muslim." It seems likely that the verse does not intend the word "Muslim" to refer merely in its sectarian sense but to Bible reading monotheists in general, whether or not they subscribe to all the minutiae of Islamic orthodoxy. In this case, the word "Muslim" is a very clear example of translation and a possible problem is how it can capture a call to unity rather than submerging in verbiage that suggests its opposite. If the translator that takes the literal meaning, as most of the translators did in the current available English translations of the Quran, then the meaning suggests the group identities of segregation or conflict. As explained above, when one really focuses on the contextual meaning one can clearly realize that the goal of this verse is to establish commonality and unity rather than forming group identities.

Here, "Tawalla" is used to mean "rejecting the message" as a unit shift in syntax. With these meanings, there is the message of conclusive approach of the communication, with the expression "Fain" meaning that "After all" as explicitness in pragmatic methodology.[37] On the other hand, "bear witness" is not a commonly used English phrase. "Be a witness" fits better in the TL as a way of phrase structure change in syntax. The audience is asked to testify that a speaker is accepting the message even if the audience does not accept it. With this in mind, a possible translation from ST to TL could be:

> After all, if they reject this message then tell them "Be our witness that we are accepting this message as Muslims do."

Or preferably with the exegetical meaning of monotheism for the word "Muslim," and the cultural filtering the translation in TL could be:

After all, if they reject this message then tell them "Be our witness that we submit ourselves to one God."

Combining all the above analysis, the article glosses the verse this way:

> *Inform all Christians and Jews and other followers of a scripture about this amazing fact!*
> *Please pay attention followers of the earlier revelations!*
> *Let's get together and realize the values that you and we hold in common!*
> *Among these values, primarily, is:*
> *We worship only to God. We should not worship anything except our same and common Creator.*[109]
> *This is because; we should not ascribe any equal with God.*
> *And therefore, we should not consider human beings as divine.*
> *We believe that only God is divine.*
> *After all, if they reject this message then tell them:*
> *"Be our witness that we submit ourselves to one God"*

This article has reviewed and analyzed different glosses to arrive at the above final version. There is a conventional method of meticulous microanalysis of sacred texts in Islam (i.e., usūl at-tafsīr or al-hadīth) which this article has not *fully* but may be partially implemented in the examination of the studied verse. For example, in the full analysis of exegetical meanings (at-tafsīr), if the focus is to understand the expression, first the words of the expressions are analyzed linguistically. Then, the meanings of the verse are analyzed within the verse with the words coming before and after it. Then, the previous verses, *siyāq*, and the verses after, *sibāq*, are analyzed to understand the primary contextual meaning. Then, the chapters making up the verses are analyzed before and after that specific verse. There may be interpretations due to the location and time of the revelation of the verse. The "reason of revelation," *asbab nuzul*, is added in the interpretation. The same expressions in other parts of the Quran are analyzed to understand how the same expressions are used. The analyst draws upon the hadith literature for the same

---

109. The Arabic reader will note that "That we only worship to God" is inserted in the translation to give an exegetical complementary meaning to the following part "We should not worship anything except to our Same and Common Creator."

contextual meanings, the literature of Arab poetry, and writings for the additional possible meanings and the literature of classical exegesis for comparison (*qiyās*). Afterward, hermeneutical analysis continues by evaluating early interpretations by the companions (*sahabah*) of the Prophet Muhammad and the canonized understandings of the Quran among the famous jurists. Future researchers could address all these possibilities. The goal is to understand and give the possible meanings of the expression in the verse with a thorough overview of the literature within the framework of Islamic scholarship, and finally, translate these possible meanings amid the objective of equivalence from the source language of Arabic to the target language of English.

Concluding Remarks for the Preferred Methodology of Translation

Lay readers rarely have access to scriptural scholar. Blame is habitually given to the monotheistic religions and their sacred texts for the conflicts that we face today. One can ask: What should we do in a world occupied with humans with different theologies, beliefs, cultural practices, physical appearances, and social norms? How do we establish a consensus that people with these differences are still to be respected, and can freely and peacefully live in a society together?

With the concern of reacting to these questions, this article has reviewed the English translations of the verse [3:64], many times referred to as the "dialogue verse," in the chapter of Imran (Father of Mary). Some of the available popular translations have differences in syntax, semantics, and pragmatic methodologies which may alter the meaning from SL to TL and form obscurity for the reader.

An emphasis on pragmatic translation[37] could accurately reflect the design embedded meanings in the Quranic verses. A lack of these sensibilities in the translation can promote conflict between theologies and groups that need to exist today.

For the purpose of the English reader, I believe that the pragmatic approach of translation optimizing the equivalence concerns in the methodology of translation is vital. It is possible that the translators may choose the similar syntactic and semantic approaches drawing upon each other's translations. Therefore, in the above-preferred translation of the verse, my effort has been combining the exegetical meanings to clarify for the reader in TL by primarily using the pragmatic approaches.[37] That does not mean that the syntactic and semantic meanings of the verse are not important. The ideal translation, I think, should prioritize the exegetical meanings through pragmatic methods.[37] Subsequently, the translator could have the concern of keeping the syntactic and semantic meanings and be concerned about the "internal rhythm" (eloquence) of the Quran in syntax and semantics by choosing proper words such as rhyming with the previous word or verse or giving the different meanings of awe, astonishment, or happiness or giving convoluted and deeper meanings with homonymy as in the text of the original Arabic revelation of the Quran that can complement all of them. Therefore, I sympathize with the translator when she/he realizes all these properties in the original text of the Quran but is not able to transfer them to the English language, especially when there is any case of a sacred text believed to be revealed from a Divine source.

BIBLIOGRAPHY

[1] Hackett, M. L. A. C. "Pew Research Center," 6 April 2017. http://www.pewresearch.org/fact-tank/2017/04/06/why-muslims-are-the-worlds-fastest-growing-religious-group/. Accessed 26 June 2018.

[2] Adamson, P. *Philosophy in the Islamic World*. Oxford University Press, 2016.

[3] Usmani, T. *An Approach to the Quranic Sciences*. Adam Publishers, 2006.

[4] Pickthall, M. W. E. *Holy Quran*. Kutub Khana Isha'at-ul-Islam, 1977.

[5] Ali, A. Y. *The meaning of the glorious Quran*. Islamic Books, 1938.

[6] Hanbal, A. B. *Musnad Imam Ahmad Ibn Hanbal*. Dar-Us-Salam Publications, 2012.

[7] Musaad, W. *Rihla 2018*. 3 July 2018.

[8] Armstrong, K. *Muhammad: A Biography of the Prophet*. Phoenix, 2001.

[9] Ramadan, T. *In the Footsteps of The Prophet*. Oxford, 2007.

[10] Al-Bukhari, M. *The Translation of the Meanings of Sahih Al-Bukhari*. Kazi Publications, 1986.

[11] Siddiqui, A. *Sahih Muslim*. Peace Vision, 1972.

[12] Cornell, V. *Voices of Islam*. Praeger Publishers, 2007.

[13] Asad, M. *The Message of the Quran: Translated and Explained*. Al-Andalus Gibraltar, 1980.

[14] Tarakci, M. & S. S. "The Quranic View of the Corruption of the Torah and the Gospels." *Islamic Quarterly*, vol. 49, no. 3, 2005, p. 227.

[15] Ernst, C. W. *How to Read the Quran: A New Guide, with Select Translations*. The University of North Carolina Press, 2011.

[16] As-Suyuti, J. *Gateway to the Quranic Sciences*. Turath Publishing, 2017.

[17] Hanson, Y. H. *Rihla Lecture Series 2018*. 5 July 2018.

[18] Hanson, Y. H. "The Creed of Imam Al-Tahawi." Zaytuna Institute, California, 2007.

[19] Addaraqutni, A. *Sunan Ad-Daraqutni*, Dar Ibn Hazm.

[20] Schimmel, A. *And Muhammad is His Messenger: The Veneration of the Prophet in Islamic Piety*. UNC Press Books, 2014.

[21] Al-Maliki, M. I. A. *Muhammad the Perfect Man*. Visions of Reality Books, 2012.

[22] Khan, F. *Rihla Lecture Series 2018*. 5 July 2018.

[23] SInternational. *The Quran*. Abul-Qasim Publishing House, 1997.

[24] Kumek, Y. J. *Practical Mysticism: Sufi Journeys of Heart and Mind*. Kendall Hunt Publishing Company, 2018.

[25] Vahide, S. *The Collection of Light*. ihlas nur publication, 2001.

[26] Tirmizi, M. *Jami At-Tirmizi*. Dar-us-Salam, 2007.

[27] Esposito, J. L. *What Everyone Needs to Know about Islam*. Oxford University Press, 2011.

[28] Griffith, S. *The Church in the Shadow of the Mosque: Christians and Muslims in the World of Islam (Jews, Chrsitians, and Muslims from the Ancient to the Modern World)*. Princeton University Press, 2012.

[29] Ajibah, A. B. *The Book of Ascension to the Essential Truths of Sufism*. Fonts Vitae, 2011.

[30] Elsadda, H. "Discourses on Women's Biographies and Cultural Identity: Twentieth-Century Representations of the Life of 'A'isha Bint Abi Bakr." *Feminist Studies*, vol. 27, no. 1, 2001, pp. 37–64.

[31] Barlas, A. *"Believing Women" in Islam: Unreading Patriarchal Interpretations of the Quran*. University of Texas Press, 2003.

[32] Sultuan, S. N. *The Quran and Sayings of Prophet Muhammad*. skylight paths publishing, 2007.

[33] Rahman, F. *Islam and Modernity: Transformation of an Intellectual Tradition*. University of Chicago Press, 1984.

[34] Majah, I. *Sunan Ibn-i-Majah*. Kitab Bhavan, 2000.

[35] Sardar, Z. *The Touch of Midas: Science, Values, and Environment in Islam and the West*. Manchester University Press, 1984.

[36] Kumek, Y. J. *Perils of Translation: Text and Behavior "A Common Word Among Us" in the Quran [3:64]*. Unpublished manuscript, 2017.

[37] Chesterman, A. *Memes of Translation*. John Benjamins Publishing Company, 1997, p. 93.

[38] Miroslow Volf, G. b. M. a. M. Y. *A Common Word*. Wm. B. Eerdmans Publishing Co., 2010.
[39] As-Suyuti, J. *Tafsir Al-Quran Al-Azim (Commentary on the Quran)*. Dar ul Fikr, 1998.
[40] Osman, S. "Iqra," 24 June 2002. http://www.iqra.net/names/QuranNames.html. Accessed 2018.
[41] Seyyed Hossein Nasr, *The Study Quran: A New Translation and Commentary*. HarperCollins, 2015.
[42] Div. Yale, "Yale Center for Faith & Culture," 24 July 2008. http://faith.yale.edu/common-word/2008-conference. Accessed 19 September 2016.
[43] Crone, P. "Jewish Christianity and the Quran." *Journal of Near Eastern Studies*, 2010, pp. 225–53.
[44] Yildirim, S. *Quran & Its Translation with Commentary*. Feza, 1998, p. 57.
[45] Munday, J. *The Routledge Companion to Translation Studies*. Routledge, 2009, p. 52.
[46] Amjad, F. A. "Problems and Strategies in English Translation of Quranic Divine Names." *International Journal of Linguistics*, 2013, pp. 128–42.
[47] Jones, F. R. "On Aboriginal Sufferance: A Process Model of Poetic Translating." *Target*, 1989, pp. 183–99.
[48] Macfarquhar, N. "New York Times," 12 October 2007. www.nytimes.com/2007/10/12/us/12muslims.html?&_r=0. Accessed 19 September 2016.
[49] BBC. "BBC News," 12 October 2007. [Online]. news.bbc.co.uk/2/hi/europe/7038992.stm. Accessed 19 September 2016.
[50] Njeru, M. V. "Are Translators Traitors? A Philosophical Perspective of Loss and Gain in Translation." *Global Journal of Human-Social Science*, vol. 15, no. 8, 2015, pp. 2249–60.
[51] Toorawa, S. "Hapless Hapaxes and Luckless Rhymes: The Quran as Literature." *Religion & Literature*, vol. 41, 2009, pp. 221–27.
[52] Ekin, Y. Kur'an Tercüme Teknikleri (Tecniques of Translating the Quran), Işık Yayıncılık Ticaret, 2015.
[53] Mir, Mustansir. "The Quran as Literature." *Religion & Literature*, 1988: 49–64.
[54] Mir, Mustansir. "Dialogue in the Quran." *Religion and Literature*, 1992: 1–22.

[55] Abu-Zayd, Nasr. "The Dilemma of the Literary Approach to the Quran." *Journal of Comparative Poetics*, 2003: 8–47.

[56] P. Rietbroek, "Brill's simple Arabic transliteration system," *Brill*, 2010.

[57] Razi, M. *Mafatih al-Ghayb known as al-Tafsir al-Kabir*. Dar Ibya al-Kutub al-Bahiyya, 1172.

[58] Khan, W. *Quran: A Simple English Translation*. Goodword, 2013.

[59] As-Sabuni, A. *Rawai'u al-Bayan Tafsir ayat al-Ahkam Min al-Qur'an*. Beirut, 1983.

[60] Kasir, I. *Tafsir al-Quran al-Azim*. Dar al-Ilm, 1982.

[61] Speight, R. M. *Interreligious documents: Guidelines for Dialogue between Christians and Muslims*. Paulist Press, 1990.

[62] Cornell, V. J. e. a. *Do Jews, Christians, and Muslims Worship the Same God?* Abingdon Press, 2012.

[63] Arberry, A. *Interpretation of Koran*. Macmillan, 1955.

[64] Senapati, B. P. *Jesus the Kalimatullah: A Christian-Muslim Relation*. Cambridge Press, 2009.

[65] Gunton, C. E. *The Cambridge Companion to Christian Doctrine*. Cambridge University Press, 1997, pp. 78, 124, & 127.

[66] Malak, A. *Muslim Narratives and the Discourse of English*. SUNY Press, 2007.

[67] Demirci, M. *Tefsir Tarihi (History of Exegesis of Quran)*. ifav, 2010, pp. 34–38.

[68] U. P. Oxford, "Oxford Dictionaries," 2016. http://www.oxforddictionaries.com/us/definition/american_english/say. Accessed 2016.

[69] Anjum, Z. *Iqbal: The Life of a Poet, Philosopher and Politician*. Random House India, 2014.

[70] Sells, M. *Approaching the Quran: The Early Revelation*. White Cloud Press, 1999.

[71] Al-Marghinani, B. F. *Al-Hidayah: The Guidance*. Amal Press, 2006.

GLOSSARY

A'bd   worshipper, servant, or slave

Accountability   liability, especially in Islam and in Abrahamic traditions, everyone has a free will or agency in this world but accountability for their actions in the afterlife in front of God

Adab   good manners, especially in the relationship with God in Sufism

Adjective   attribute, a phrase describing a noun

Adonai   name of God in Judaism

Affair   relationship

Agency   acting as an agent or a carrier with free will

Alhamdulillah   a chanted divine phrase of appreciation of God or Allah

Alienating   isolating, separating, disconnecting

Alienating Images of God   understandings about God that disconnects person to establish a regular relationship with the Divine or to follow a religion

Allah   proper name of God in Islam

Allude   explain, refer

Anger   uncontrolled and chaotic human spiritual state

Aphorism   sayings, proverbs in a culture, society, or belief

Appreciate   thank

Appreciative   with capital A, God

Arabic   language, especially the language of revelation of the Quran

Arrogance   feelings and actions of superiority

Ascension rising, especially in Sufism, increase of spiritual states in relationship with God

Assert claim

Astagfirullah a divine phrase of asking forgiveness from God and cleaning the heart

Attribute adjective, a phrase describing a noun, especially in Sufism

Attributes of God divine phrases describing God

Authentic original, genuine, true

Balance modesty, especially in Sufism, following the middle way

Behavior temporary nature of a person

Bismillah a divine phrase of starting something with the blessing of God

Book of Chant the Quran

Boost increase

Bowing down bending one's body, especially the act of respect by bending one's body, for God

Caution carefulness, alertness, especially in Sufism, in spiritual manners not to be trapped by ego or self

Certainty knowing without doubt, especially in Sufism, knowing and experiencing without doubt

Chanting repeating, especially in Sufism, repeating the phrases with focus and experience

Chaos disorder and confusion, especially in Sufism (spiritual) chaos being in negative states of anxiety, stress, and purposelessness

Charge positive states of spirituality that makes the person happy, peaceful, and calm, filling oneself with divine knowledge and experience

Compassion loving and caring

Confirming Book the Quran

Confirming Scripture the Quran

Conscience   internal instinct of distinguishing right or wrong

Consciousness   awareness

Constant   not changing, permanent, especially in practice, known as Reflective Attributes of God, where humans have an image but God has its source

Construction   formation of an abstract entity

Contract   squeeze

Convergence   similarity

Cosmology   knowledge about the origin and development of the universe

Covenant   agreement

Death   end of physical faculties of a person, especially physical versus spiritual death; the soul does not die but the body dies in understanding of physical death in Islam

Dedication   sincere constant effort

Deity   representation of the transcendent

Detox   discharge

Devout   pious, practicing

Dhikr   as one of the names of the Quran, or any type of chant to remember God

Discharge   negative states of spirituality that makes the person sad, stressed, and anxious, especially in Sufism, emptying oneself from all the temporal and worldly positive and negative attachments

Divine   transcendent

Doctrine   teaching

Dominance   control

Dream   visions when one is sleeping or awake

Ego   self, identifier of a person, especially in Sufism, raw and uneducated identifier and controller of a person

Elohim name of God in Judaism

Embodiment, versus embody making it part of one's character

Endeavor engagement, activities

Epistemology theory of knowledge

Ethical moral

Ethnographic based on observation

Etiquette good manners and respect, especially in Sufism, respect in the relationship with God

Evil anything that causes stress, sadness, or anxiety

Evil eye the belief of unknown effects of the human eye across different cultures, traditions, and religions; especially in Sufism the evil eye effects due to extreme hatred, jealousy, or oppositely, evil eye effects due to extreme veneration and love of someone

Expand enlarge

Experience internalization of knowledge

Experience or experiential knowledge all types of learning except from a book or a teacher, internalizing and personalizing the formal learning

Figurative unclear, secondary and metaphorical

Free Will free choice of a person in decision-making

Generous with capital G, God

Genre type

Genuine sincere, original, authentic

Ghazali philosopher, theologian, Sufi mystic, lived in twelfth century

Glorification the mental, spiritual, and maybe verbal act of describing God in an admirable way

Groundless fake

Habitual habit of doing something constantly

GLOSSARY

HasbiyaAllah a chant with a meaning of "God is sufficient for me"

Heaven a place of all maximized pleasures of bodily and spiritual engagements while being with God

Hell a place of punishment

Humbleness behavior of modesty in viewing oneself, accepting the weakness in one's relationship with God and not being disrespectful and arrogant to God

Humility character or trait of humbleness

Illa Allah "except Allah" or "except God"

Images of God understandings and experiences about God

Imitation trying without real understanding

Infinite God, the Unlimited

Informant a person who participates in anthropological research

InshAllah God willing, hopefully

Intention planning ideas before the action

Intrinsic internal

Islam name of a religion that emphasizes believing in one God and Jesus, Moses, and Muhammad to be the human prophets of the Creator

Jihad struggle, especially spiritual struggle within oneself

Joseph Prophet of God in Islam, Christianity, and Judaism

Journey struggles of following guidelines of a mystical school

Khidr mystical being who is sent by God at any time to help people in their problems; also believed to be the teacher of Moses in a mystical journey as mentioned in the Quran

Kitab the Quran

Knowledge theoretical understanding of something through education

La ilaha illa Allah there is no God except Allah, a critical Divine phrase of chanting in Sufism implying a spiritual charge and discharge

Literal clear and primary

Lord God

Lucifer Satan, mentioned in divine scriptures such as the Bible and the Quran

Majnun crazy or, especially in Sufism, heretic

Mantra a repetitive phrase or sound, especially used in Hinduism and Buddhism

Meditation deep focus especially with reflection

Memorization learning by heart

Mercy compassion and forgiveness

Middle way living a balanced life in spiritual and worldly engagements

Mimic imitate

Mind logic, reason, and rationality

Miracle incidents against the law of physics and against all natural sciences

Mosque temple of Muslims

Muhammad the Prophet of Islam

Musaddiq the Quran

Mystic a person who adopts the teachings of mysticism

Mysticism the knowledge of the transcendent

Nafs self in its raw form

Neat tidy and in order

Negation denial, emptying from the mind and heart the imperfect ideas and feelings about God

Neglectful not giving the proper attention that is due

Notion concept, idea

Odd not even, unique, no equivalence

One with capital denoting the one and only Creator

Oppression unjust action of the strong over the weak

Permanent constant, not changing, not ending

Permanent non-ending

Phenomenon occurrence

Pious devout, practicing

Pollution making something dirty

Pronunciation correct sounds of letters in a language

Prostration, versus to prostrate the act of respect by putting one's face on the ground, humbling oneself for God by putting the face, the noble part of the body, on the ground

Qibla the direction where Muslims turn when they pray

Quran sacred text of Muslims

Rabbinic related to the Rabbis, the priests, and teachers of Judaism

Recitation, versus to recite reading, versus to read

Reliance dependence

Repetition repeating

Reverence respect

Reward prize, payment, especially in worldly and afterlife rewards in Islam

Ritual practices in a religion or mysticism that have spiritual and divine value for a person

Ruku bowing down

Rumi great Sufi mystic

Saint the person who believed to be close to God

Sakina peaceful and calm feelings

Salawat names of the chants to remember teachers and their covenants with their students, especially the main teacher, the Prophet Muhammad and others, such as Abraham, Moses, and Jesus

Samad the One who does not need anything, but everyone and everything needs God

Satan the Devil, Lucifer, mentioned in divine scriptures such as in the Bible and the Quran

Scent perfume, nice smell

Scholar expert, the experts who practice what they teach (alim)

Scripture sacred book or sacred text

Self ego, identifier of a person, raw and uneducated identifier and controller of a person

Service ethical action of doing good for others and society

Spiritual Journey struggles of following guidelines of a mystical school

State level, especially in Sufism, spiritual level

Struggle efforts to achieve a goal

SubhanAllah glorification of God, a divine phrase of chanting of spirituality implying a spiritual charge and discharge

SubhanAllahu wa bihamdihi a divine phrase of glorification of God

SubhanAllahul Azeem a divine phrase of glorification of God in the prostration posture

SubhanRabbiyalAzim phrase of glorification for God in the bowing posture

Submission natural acceptance of the uncontrolled and unseen

Sufi follower of Sufism

Sufism mystical path of Islam

Superstitious fake

Surrender involuntary state of acceptance of the uncontrolled and the unseen

Tahajjud night prayer

GLOSSARY

Talismanic unknown and indescribable effects of divine words and sounds

Taqwa respect of God

Temple worship place

Temporal transitory

Temptation false ideas

The Curer God

The Divine God

The Forgiver a name of God in Islam

The Friend a name of God in Islam

The Helper a name of God in Islam

The Lover a name of God in Islam

The Peace Giver God

The Real God

The Real Maker God

The Reminder the Quran

The Source God

The Sustainer a name of God in Sufism

The Wise with capital W, God

Throne a figurative or metaphorical representation of dominion of God

Trait permanent character or nature

Tranquility peace and calmness

Transcendent beyond human limits

Transitory temporal

Transliteration writing the sounds of words or phrases in one language with an alphabet of another language

Union being together, especially in this book, goal and joy of being always in the presence of God

Unseen anything five senses cannot testify in scientific methods

Weak not having a physical strength to perform an action, especially in Sufism, not having spiritual strength to perform any action

Worshipper a person who regularly follows and practices rituals, acts of prayers

ACKNOWLEDGMENTS

I would like to thank all my unnamed teachers, friends, and students for their input, ideas, suggestions, help, and support during and before the preparation of this book.

I would like to thank Professor David Banks, faculty of the Department of Anthropology, State University of New York (SUNY) at Buffalo, for meeting with me daily to go over the manuscript. I would like to thank Mufti Asim of Darul Uloom Al-Madania of Buffalo, Sheikh Ali of Hartford Seminary, Sheikh Tamer of Jami Masjid for all their valuable suggestions.

Lastly, I would like to thank all of my family members for their patience with me during the preparation of this book.

ABOUT THE AUTHOR

Dr. Yunus J. Kumek is currently teaching at Harvard Divinity School on Islam. He has been religious studies coordinator at State University of New York (SUNY) Buffalo State and teaching undergraduate and graduate courses in religious studies at SUNY at Buffalo State, Niagara University and Daemen College. Before becoming interested in religious studies, Dr. Kumek was doing his doctorate degree in physics at SUNY at Buffalo published academic papers in the areas of quantum physics, and medical physics. Then, he decided to engage with the world of social sciences through social anthropology, education, and cultural anthropology in his doctorate studies. He later spent a few years as a research associate in the anthropology department of the same university and published a book about different cultures and beliefs of international teachers in America. Recently, he completed a postdoctoral fellowship at Harvard Divinity school and published books on religious literacy through ethnography and practical mysticism: Sufi journeys of heart and mind. Dr. Kumek had classical training in Islamic sciences from the teachers of Egypt, India, Turkey, Yemen, Somalia, Morocco, and the United States. He stayed and studied in Egypt and Turkey. Dr. Kumek, who remains interested in physics—solves physics problems to relax—enjoys different languages, German, Spanish, Arabic, Hebrew, Urdu, and Turkish, especially in his research of scriptural analysis. Dr. Kumek takes great pleasure in classical poetry as well.

INDEX

A

Abraham, 2, 7, 11, 16, 17, 18, 19, 24, 25
Abuse, 127
Accountability, 130, 143
Adam, 24, 25, 34, 35, 72
Advice, 165
Afterlife, 10, 27, 36, 37
Allah, 2, 3, 5, 14, 15, 68, 78, 97, 102, 132, 145, 149, 150, 154, 160, 189, 208, 112
American Muslims, 2, 37, 38
Angels, 19, 26, 139, 140
Animals, 111, 196
Appreciation, 136
Appreciation of God, 136, 194
Arabic Language, 13, 90, 139
Arrogance, 112, 209
Art, 49
Atom's weight, 206
Attributes of God, 3
Authenticity, 10, 12
Authenticity of the Quran, 12
Ayatul Kursi, 68

B

Backbiting, 159
Bee, 96
Beginning of Islam, 2

Belief, 101
Bible, 10, 66, 67, 70, 79, 82
Biblical Narratives, 18
Birds, 116, 169
Buddha, 7

C

Calligraphy, 49
Cat Stevens, 37, 38
Certainty, 209
Chanting, 10
Chapter of Ikhlas, 5, 6
Chapter of Sincerity, 5, 6
Charity, 34
Cheating, 187
Chest, 135, 200
Child Education, 124
Christianity, 11, 36, 37
Christians, 11, 205
Classifications, 147
Clergy, 10
Common Word, 73
Compulsion in religion, 88
Conflict, 85
Confucius, 7
Core of Islam, 16
Core of Islamic Faith, 16
Cosmology, 109
Creation process, 107, 190, 202

Creator, 14, 15
Critical Thinking, 171

D

Daily Prayers, 31, 32, 33
Day, 221
Day of Judgment, 126, 221
Death, 27, 148, 163
Deception, 186
Declaration of Faith, 29
Deity, 2
Destiny, 28, 29
Dhikr, 100
Dialogue, 216
Different Attributes of God, 4, 15
Different Attributes of Allah, 4, 15
Different Names of Allah, 4, 15
Different Names of God, 4, 15
Disbelief, 101
Divine Scriptures, 24, 25
Divinity, 20, 219
Divorce, 166
Dr. Oz, 37, 38

E

Education, 49, 203
Embryo, 107, 131, 190
End of Days, 182, 185, 188
Environmental Pollution, 122
Ethics, 98
Ethnic groups, 147
European Muslims, 37, 38
Evil, 28, 74, 76, 84, 99, 198, 206, 229
Evil-eye, 170

F

Failure, 195
Faith Pillars of Islam, 14
Family Life, 47, 122, 144
Fantasy, 152
Fasting, 33
Finances and divorce, 166
Fingerprints, 178
Five Times Daily Prayers, 31, 32, 33
Food, 50
Freedom, 47
Friendship, 161

G

Gabriel, 19, 26
Gender, 46, 44, 45
Gender Identity, 47
Glorification, 100
God, 2, 3, 5, 14, 15, 68, 78, 97, 102, 132, 145, 149, 150, 154, 160, 189, 208, 112
God's Communication, 140
Good, 28
Gospel, 10, 11, 24, 25, 66, 67, 70, 79, 82
Greeting, 77
Guidance, 66, 67

H

Hadith, 9
Hajj, 34
Halal, 50
Happy Self, 193
Heart, 135, 146, 158, 177, 191, 200

Heaven, 27, 28
Holy Sites, 212, 213
Honor, 47
Human Being, 179
Humanness of the Prophet, 8
Humbleness, 129, 138, 139
Humility, 129, 138, 139
Husband, 122

I

Identities, 147
Illusion, 152
Iman, 14
Individual Rights, 47
Injil, 3, 24, 25
Islam, 2
Islam in the West, 37, 38
Islamic Law, 41
Islamic Philosophy, 27

J

Jesus, 2, 3, 7, 11, 16, 18, 19, 36, 37, 72, 104
Jews, 205
Jihad, 27
Jinn, 175
JJ, 3
Jonah, 18
Joseph, 91
Judaism, 11, 36, 37
Judeo-Christian, 18

K

Kabah, 34, 35, 212, 213
Kareem Abdul-Jabbar, 37, 38
Kind words, 93
Kindness, 93

Kinship Relations, 144
Knowledge of God, 6

L

Language of the Quran, 90
Learning, 203
Life after Death, 27
Life of Muhammad, 7, 8
Life of the Prophet Muhammad, 7
Lot, 11

M

Manual, 106
Marifatullah, 5
Mary, 11, 16, 167, 168
Meanness, 211
Memorization, 13
Memorization of the Quran, 13
Mercy of God, 208
Messengership, 19
Methodology of Translation, 61
Michael, 19, 26
Mike Tyson, 37, 38
Milk, 96
Miracle of the Quran, 12
Miracles, 17, 20
Miracles in Islam, 20
Monogamy, 46
Monotheism, 14, 15, 219
Moon, 154
Moses, 2, 7, 11, 16, 18, 19
Mu'min, 14
Muhammad, 7, 19
Muhammad Ali, 37, 38
Muslims Belief, 14

N

Names of Chapters, 54
Names of God, 3
Night of Power, 204
Nights, 176, 197, 221
Noah, 18

O

Old age, 123

P

Parent Rights, 144
Permissible, 50
Pilgrimage, 34
Politics, 41
Pollution, 122
Polygamy, 46
Prayer, 64, 65, 214
Prayer Beads, 44
Property, 47
Prophet Muhammad, 7, 19
Prophet Muhammad's Character, 20
Prophet Muhammad's Miracles, 20
Prophethood, 19
Prophets, 2, 18, 19
Prostration, 112
Protection, 221, 222
Psalms, 10, 11, 24, 25, 66, 67, 70, 79, 82
Purpose, 109
Purpose of Miracles, 17

Q

Quran, 9, 12, 66, 77, 92, 101, 103, 105, 121, 139, 153, 181

R

Rabb, 64, 65
Reflection, 171
Refuge, 221, 222
Religion and Wealth, 118
Reminder, 192
Revelation, 70
Rumi, 43

S

Salah, 31, 32, 33, 214
Salah, 214
Satan, 133, 134
Sawm, 33
Science, 49
Scientific Arrogance, 137
Scriptures, 24, 25
Self, 106, 193
Self-Accountability, 125
Shahadah, 29, 30
Shelter, 221, 222
Signs of the End of Days, 142
Slander, 211
Social Ethics, 47
Social groups, 147
Sperm, 107, 190
Sperm and Egg, 107, 190
Spouse, 122
Stars, 156
Straight Path, 138, 64, 65
Struggle, 89, 94, 119, 120
Success, 195
Sufi, 43
Sufism, 42
Sun, 154
Sunrise, 112
Sunset, 112

Surah Fatiha, 64, 65
Surah Ikhlas, 5, 6, 219
Surahs, 54
SWT, 3

T

Taqwa, 67
Tarawih, 33
Tasawwuf, 42
Tasbih, 44
Tawrah, 24, 25
Tazkiya, 120
the Active, 68
the Alive, 68
the Book, 66
the Forever, 68
the Friend, 69
the Gospel, 3, 10, 11, 24, 25, 66, 67, 70, 79, 82
The Merciful, 154
The Opening, 64, 65
the Permanent, 68
the Prophet, 7, 19
the Psalms, 10, 11, 24, 25, 66, 67, 70, 79, 82
the Quran, 9, 12, 66, 77, 92, 101, 103, 105, 121, 139, 153, 181
the Torah, 3, 10, 11, 24, 25, 66, 67, 70, 79, 82
Time, 210
Tolerance, 216
Torah, 3, 10, 11, 24, 25, 66, 67, 70, 79, 82

Transgression, 48
Translation, 13, 61
Translation of the Quran, 13
Transliteration, 61
Trinity, 36, 37

U

Ungratefulness, 207
Unseen Beings, 175

V

Violence, 39
Virgin Mary, 11, 16, 167, 168

W

Whirling Dervishes, 43
Wife, 122
Wife of Pharaoh, 167
Wine, 156
Women, 44, 45, 46
Worship, 29, 164
Worship Pillars, 29

Y

Yusuf, 91

Z

Zabur, 24, 25
Zakah, 34
Zulm, 48

www.ingramcontent.com/pod-product-compliance
Lightning Source LLC
Chambersburg PA
CBHW071736150426
43191CB00010B/1598